Benjamin J. K. Anderson

**Narrative of a journey to Musardu**

the capital of the western Mandingoes

Benjamin J. K. Anderson

**Narrative of a journey to Musardu**
*the capital of the western Mandingoes*

ISBN/EAN: 9783744745635

Printed in Europe, USA, Canada, Australia, Japan

Cover: Foto ©Andreas Hilbeck / pixelio.de

More available books at **www.hansebooks.com**

# NARRATIVE

OF A

# JOURNEY TO MUSARDU,

THE

CAPITAL OF THE WESTERN MANDINGOES.

BY

BENJAMIN ANDERSON.

New-York:
S. W. GREEN, PRINTER, 16 AND 18 JACOB STREET.
1870.

# INTRODUCTION.

SMITHSONIAN INSTITUTION, January, 1870.

IT had long been considered important by the friends of Liberia that an exploration should be made of the country east of the Republic. The only difficulty in the way was to find the proper man for the enterprise. President Warner had for a number of years been seeking for such a one, when the author of the accompanying narrative volunteered to undertake the exploration. He is a young man, educated in Liberia, of pure negro blood, and had previously served as Secretary of the Treasury under President Warner. The narrative is printed without correction from the original manuscript, and the principal portion of the edition has been presented to the Smithsonian Institution by Mr. H. Maunsell Schieffelin, for distribution.

JOSEPH HENRY,
*Secretary Smithsonian Institution.*

# INDEX.

| | PAGE |
|---|---|
| Leaves Monrovia, | 9 |
| Exploration Obstructed, | 11, 17, 47 |
| Vaunswah, | 12, 23 |
| Leopards Numerous, | 12 |
| Bessa's and its Walls, | 15, 23 |
| Iron Ore, | 14, 105, 111 |
| " Used for Shot, | 39 |
| " Polished Walk, | 83 |
| " Smelting, | 84 |
| " Working, | 110 |
| Boozie Savage Warriors, | 17 |
| Slave Trade, | 21, 39, 109 |
| " Insurrection, | 41 |
| Boporu, | 22, 26 |
| Totoquella, | 28 |
| Stereoscope, | 33, 45 |
| Salt for Settling Fueds, | 30 |
| Bessa Compelled to Restore, | 36 |
| St. Paul's River Falls, | 39 |
| Momora wants a School, | 45 |
| Good for a Mission Station, | 45 |
| Arabic Grammar, | 40 |
| " Reading and Writing, | 107 |
| Fish Plenty, | 44, 117 |
| Cotton Weaving and Dyeing, | 44, 56, 61, 79. |
| Agriculture, | 85, 105 |
| Rice, Cotton, Tobacco, etc., | 56, 61, 65, 105. |
| Cane and Plantains, | 86 |
| Zelleki, | 50 |
| Dallazeah, | 51 |
| Zolu's, | 53 |
| Zow Zow, | 54 |

| | PAGE |
|---|---|
| Markets, | 44, 54, 67, 79, 109 |
| Religion, | 40 |
| Religious Toleration, | 107, 110 |
| Convent for Women, | 68 |
| Handsome Green Stone, | 58 |
| Fissabue, | 63 |
| Bokkasah, | 64 |
| King Dowilnyah, | 71 |
| His Cruelty, | 72 |
| War Dance, | 75 |
| Fear of Instruments, | 76 |
| Ziggah Porrah Zue, | 77 |
| Bridge over St. Paul's, | 80 |
| Elephants plenty, | 83 |
| " for Dinner, | 117 |
| Music, | 18, 31, 78, 81. 90 |
| Sheep, Cattle, Horses, | 83, 100, 104, 109 |
| Ballatah, | 83 |
| Vukkah, | 85 |
| Mahommadu, | 87 |
| Musardu, | 88 |
| " Healthy and Dry, | 91 |
| " Cavalry, (1500;) Military Exhibition, | 93 |
| Harmattan Dust, | 108 |
| Musardu Oppressed | 95 |
| " Expecting War, | 99 |
| Gold, | 95, 100, 101 |
| Poison for Arrows, | 103 |
| Hawks and Strange Bird, | 106 |
| Expected Attack, | 113 |
| Population, | 39, 66, 84, 91, 107, 113 |
| Mandingo Dress, | 91 |
| Trading Forts Recommended, | 100 |

# A JOURNEY TO MUSARDU.

This account of a journey to Musardu, the capital of the Western Mandingoes, is the result of a proposal made by Mr. Henry M. Schieffelin, of New-York, through President D. B. Warner, of Liberia, who for six or eight years had been endeavoring, till now without success, to induce the inauguration of an expedition from Liberia, to explore the interior as far as possible. Mr. Schieffelin and Caleb Swan, Esq., of New-York, furnished the means necessary to carry on the exploration.

No especial point was indicated by the promoters of this exploration; only the general direction was given, east and north-east. The especial point, however, agreed upon by my friends in Monrovia, was Musardu, the capital of the Western Mandingoes. This is the portion of the country of Manding which our citizens Seymore and Ash attempted to visit; but their travels were unfortunately interrupted in a manner that nearly cost them their lives.

The Mandingoes have always excited the liveliest interest on account of their superior physical appearance, their natural intelligence, their activity, and their enterprise. No one has passed unnoticed these tall black men from the eastern interior, in whose countenances spirit and intellect are strongly featured.

Their diligent journeys from Tallakondah have allowed no sea-coast town north-west of the St. Paul's to remain unvisited. Their avidity for trade has drawn them from their treeless plains to the Atlantic ocean. Their zeal for Islam has caused the name of Mohammed to be pronounced in this part of Africa, where it otherwise would never have been mentioned.

Musardu can, by easy journeys, be reached from Monrovia in twenty-five or thirty days. I was obliged, however, from the delays and inconveniences incident to interior traveling in Africa, to occupy thirteen months.

Sometimes I was compelled to spend considerable lengths of time in one place. I have not on that account burdened this report with insipid recitals of what, every day, nearly repeated itself. Whatever struck me as descriptive of the country, or illustrative of the manners of the people, that I have recorded.

I am sensible that the regions through which I have traveled are capable of yielding vaster stores of information, in a scientific point of view, than what I have afforded; but I shall be satisfied if this humble beginning succeeds in encouraging others in the same direction, and on a more extensive scale. I shall now proceed to narrate the journey from Monrovia to Musardu; but especially from Boporu to Musardu.

I shall rapidly march through the two grand divisions of the Boozie country. I shall first make the reader acquainted with the Domar Boozie; introduce him at once to the populous and thriving towns of Zolu, Zow-Zow, Salaghee, Fissahbue, and Bokkasaw. Leaving the Domar country, we shall enter the Wymar country, give time to rest at Ziggah Porrah Zue, in latitude 8° 14′ 45″, its capital, the vast and noisy market of which takes place every Sunday, upon the banks of the same river on which Clay Ashland, Louisiana, Virginia, and Caldwell are seated—the St. Paul's. We shall then cross that river upon a suspension bridge of wicker-work, elevated twenty-five feet from its surface, and come into the territory of one of the most warlike kings in the Wymar country, the bloody Donilnyah. We shall not tarry long in his presence; but, hastening away, nothing shall stop our progress—not even the Vukkah mountains, a boundary acknowledged to divide the fertile hills of Wymar from the almost treeless plains of Manding. Crossing these with the tramp and speed of a soldier, we shall quickly descend into the country of the Western Mandingoes; visit their principal cities; and, finally, take up our abode in their very capital—Musardu.

The instruments with which observations were made were: One sextant, by E. & G. W. Blunt, New-York; one aneroid barometer; two thermometers—1st, 133°; 2d, 140°, by B. Pike, New-York; two small night and day compasses, by H. W. Hunter, New-York; one tolerably good watch; one artificial horizon.

As for the accuracy of these calculations of latitude and longitude, whatever painstaking and the instruments enumerated above could do, has not been neglected.

I have not been able to calculate the profile of the

route according to the usual methods, because it was impossible to procure the proper instruments, with which a contemporaneous register ought to have been kept at Monrovia, during my absence.

Even the barometer with which I was furnished was an aneroid, an instrument that has to be referred from time to time to the mercurial barometer for adjustment.

I can not say that the indications of the instrument were material departures from the truth. It certainly indicated the rise and fall of land in a satisfactory and unmistakable manner, both in going to and returning from Musardu.

At Totoquella, in latitude 7° 45′ 24″, and Boporu, June 9th and 13th, it ranged 29.36, 29.34. Upon my return in March it ranged from 29.14 to 29.24. This difference may be ascribed, partly to difference of seasons of rains and dries, and partly to want of accuracy in the instrument itself.

I was not even able to ascertain directly the several heights of land by means of the boiling point of water, because my thermometers ranged only from 133° to 140° Fahrenheit. The highest rise of land was indicated by the aneroid at 27.61 inches; the boiling point of which would have been 208° Fahrenheit. See Davies & Peck's Mathematical Dictionary, page 338, "Table of barometric heights corresponding to difference of temperature of boiling water." It is from these tables that I have made approximate estimates of the elevations of land.

Taking the indications of the aneroid at the several places, and ascertaining from the tables the boiling points at each place, (which always rated higher than my two thermometers of 133° and 140° Fahrenheit,) I then made the calculation as if I had ascertained the boiling point directly from the thermometer. For example, the barometer and thermometer at Ziggah Porrah Zue stood 28.08 and 86°.

The boiling point of 28.06 (see Tables) is 208° Fah.

| | |
|---|---:|
| From Table I. for 208° height, | 2049 feet. |
| Proportional part for 0° 8', deduct | 408 |
| | 1641 |
| Multiplier from Table II. for 86°, | 1112 |
| | |
| Approximate height required, | 1824 feet. |

The number of longitudes would have been greater, had it not been for the difficulty of reading off the limb of the sextant at night.

On the 14th of February, 1868, I embarked the effects of the expedition in a large canoe, loaned me by Dr. C. B. Dunbar for the purpose. We reached Virginia, on the St. Paul's, at six o'clock P.M. The next morning we started for Vannswah, a Dey village, four and a half miles in the rear of Virginia. This village was once occupied wholly by the Deys, but their power is fast waning, and more than half the village is now in the hands of Mandingo traders from Boporu.

Here it was that I had made a previous arrangement for the conduct of the expedition, with a learned Mandingo, Kaifal-Kanda, who had lately arrived from his native town Billelah, a place near to, and scarcely second in importance to Musardu itself.

I was detained here three weeks waiting for him to arrange our departure. In the mean time all my carriers, who were Kroomen, deserted me, with the exception of their head-man, Ben; being frightened by what the Dey people told them of the dangers of the road. Kaifal at first proposed to send me direct to Boporu; but my friends at Monrovia were so apprehensive that I should not be able to pass through that country, that I refused to go to Boporu. Subsequent events proved that their apprehensions were not entirely unfounded.

Boporu, though the most direct route, or the route most usually traveled, is also the place where the strongest opposition is offered to any one wishing to pass through. It is the place where the policy of non-intercourse originated. Its power and policy dominate over the surrounding regions.

It was upon my refusal to go to Boporu that Kaifal sent me to Bessa's town, which is situated forty miles west of Boporu. And though it is somewhat independent of the authority of Momoru Son, the king of Boporu, the same practice prevails with respect to prohibiting all penetration into the interior.

Before setting out on this expedition, I made every effort to join another civilized person with me; but the undertaking was considered of too dangerous a character. I tried to prevail on some of the young men, who had but little else to do at the time; but was so entirely unsuccessful, that I fear their reputation for enterprise and hardihood must suffer when I relate how they preferred the safe, soft, grassy streets of Monrovia to an expedition into the heart of their country, simply because it was said to be perilous. I thereafter received other discouragements, from such a quarter and of such a character that I must forbear to mention them.

Many stories were rife of the unsettled state of the country: that the roads between us and the interior tribes were infested by banditti, and that war was raging between interior tribes themselves; that between all these jarring forces, it was impossible for the expedition to survive forty miles. And this was the opinion of those who were in a condition to be the best informed. But as the expedition was pushed on in the very localities where these difficulties were said to exist, it was found that there were disturbances, but not of a character to entirely prohibit our progress.

The practice of exaggerating every petty affair into the proportions of a universal war, is used for a purpose; being often an artifice to produce general consternation, out of which the more knowing may cull every advantage for themselves.

Besides, it is the policy of our intervening tribes to get up scare-crow reports, to prevent intercourse between the interior and Liberia. Nothing is more dreaded, and especially by the Boporu Mandingoes, than the penetration of the interior by the Liberians. There is, therefore, a complete line of obstruction, extending east and west, in the rear of Montserrado country, which hinders or inconveniences trade. It deserves the immediate action of government, in order that the interior trade may be completely unfettered from such annoyances.

It is along this line that the Boporu Mandingoes

and others are determined to be the "go-betweens" to the inland trade and Liberian enterprise. They it is who are chiefly engaged in making beef scarce, and country cloths small; who trammel and clog the Boozie and Barline trade.

On the 6th of March, having hired eighteen Congoes, to supply the place of the Kroomen who had deserted me, we started from Vannswah for Bessa's town, under the conduct of two of Kaifal's young men. Bessa's town was the place pitched upon as our starting-point for Musardu, since I had refused to go to Boporu.

Passing, as rapidly as our burdens would permit, the towns of Vyrmore, Sne, Moah, Weta, and Bambu, we reached Mannèenah on Thursday, the 12th of March. We had been traveling in a north-eastern direction; halting here, we saw a large mountain, north-east by east, behind which Boporu is said to lie. We had now to change our course to westward, in order to go to Bessa's town. All the towns and villages through which we had passed, except Weta, Bambu, and Mannèenah, belonged to the Deys. This tribe was once numerous and powerful, but is now scatteringly sprinkled in small and unimportant villages over the face of the country. They have a relic of their old antipathy against Liberians. Slave-trade, war, and their absorption into other tribes have nearly obliterated every thing that distinguished them as a tribe. Old Gatumba's town, both in appearance and hospitality, is the only redeeming feature in this part of the country.

In this region leopards are numerous, and sometimes

dangerous. The female leopard is particularly dangerous when she has the care of her young. It is said that leopards never attack first, and will always shun you whenever they can do so. This rule, like many others, has some exceptions, and sometimes some very fatal ones. A female leopard having her cub with her met a man in a sudden turn of the road; she flew at him, and came nigh breaking the rule entirely as to him, but for the strength of his lungs and the speed of his legs, all of which had to be brought into desperate requisition.

At Weta's town an enormous leopard was shot by an old man. As soon as he saw the mammoth cat, he was taken with the trembles; but, remembering that it was only the matter of a few moments which should have the first chance for life, he leveled his piece at the head of the crouching animal, and in an instant had the satisfaction to see that the object of his fears was stretched helpless on the earth.

This trophy of the old man's prowess was borne home in triumph, and divided into many parcels. The chine-bone is considered the bone of contention; and, as soon as it is severed from the rest, it is thrown high in the air, in order that when it comes to the ground—

"Those may take who have the power,
And those may keep who can."

A general scramble ensues, in which it is clearly proved that a part is greater than the whole; for the chine-bone can produce a greater row, and a bigger fight, than if the whole animal, instinct with its living ferocity, had jumped plump into the middle of the crowd.

The physical features of the country are roughened by hills, valleys, and small plains; and similar inequalities of surface prevail to what may be seen in the rear of Clay Ashland; indeed, the Clay Ashland hills are a part of them, and must have been produced by the same physical causes.

These hills grow bolder and more conspicuous in outline as we advance in the interior. Sometimes linked together by gentle depressions, and sometimes entirely detached from each other, they form no definite range; rising and running toward every point of the compass, they present all the varieties of figure and direction that hills can assume.

Their composition, so far as could be discerned from their surface, was the ordinary vegetable mould, with boulders of iron ore, granite, white quartz, and a mixed detritus from these various rocks, charged in many places with thin-leaved mica, similar to that which is seen in the Clay Ashland hills.

Before we reached the margin of the Boporu, or Boatswain country, we passed through long and almost unbroken strips of forests, upon a road partaking of the uneven character of the country, and strewn for miles with sharp pebbles and vitreous quartz, rendering travel painful enough to the unshodden pedestrian. Huge boulders of granite were dispersed here and there, relieving the gloom and monotony of large, shady forest trees. This region is intersected with numerous streams flowing over sandy bottoms or granite beds, with a temperature of 58°, 60°, and 62° Fahrenheit.

On Saturday, the 13th of March, we left Mannèenah, and after traveling forty miles westward, we reached Bessa's town, at six o'clock P.M. Bessa's town is in latitude 7° 3' 19", in the western portion of the Golah country. It is elevated about four hundred and eighty feet above the level of the sea. This town is located in a small, irregular plain, studded with palm-trees, and hedged in by hills in nearly every direction. It is strongly fortified with a double barricade of large wooden stakes; in the space between each barricade sharp-pointed stakes, four feet long, are set obliquely in the ground, crossing each other; this is to prevent the defenses from being scaled. The town is of an oval form; the north and south points resting on the edge of swamps; the east and west points, which are the points of access, are flanked with a strong quadrilateral stockade, with four intervening gates between the outside gate and the town itself. There are guard-houses to each of these gates, and people constantly in them night and day. To a force without artillery this town would give some trouble. It contains about three hundred and fifty clay dwellings, of various sizes, and between eight hundred and one thousand inhabitants, who may be regarded as the permanent population. Of the transient traders and visitors it would be difficult to form any estimate. The houses are huddled together in a close and most uncomfortable proximity; in some parts of the town scarcely two persons can walk abreast. In matters of cleanliness and health, King Bessa can not be said to have seriously consulted the interests of his people.

Bessa himself is a personage well known to one of our best citizens, Mr. Gabriel Moore. He is of Mandingo extraction. I regret, however, to say that he is deplorably wanting in that sedateness and religious cast of feeling which usually forms the distinguishing characteristic of that tribe.

I was informed that he had purchased a dispensation from the rigid observances of that creed from some of the Mandingo priests, by paying a large amount of money. This license to do evil so affected our journey to Musardu, that it came nearly breaking up the expedition altogether.

It was on a Friday we arrived in this town—a day said to be always inauspicious. We introduced ourselves as being sent to him by one of his own countrymen, Kaifal Kanda, a Mandingo, living at Vannswah, with whom we were going to Musardu.

He affected to listen with great attention; spoke of the commotions of the interior, which, as he said, was a great obstacle and hinderance to all traveling just at that time. He also informed me that he would have to consult the other kings behind him before allowing me to pass; and he kept on creating difficulty after difficulty, all reasonable and fair enough in argument, but point blank lies in fact. He had no consulting to do; for he was at that time at variance with the principal neighboring chiefs.

I was not pleased with my first audience, yet I was induced to make Bessa the following presents: three bars of tobacco, one double barreled pistol, one large brass kettle, one piece of fancy handkerchiefs, and one keg of powder. This gift was received with satisfaction, but it was hinted that the king was anxious to trade with me for the rest of my money. I had, therefore, to distinctly state that I did not wish to trade, as that would prevent me from accomplishing the object for which I had come, namely, to go to Musardu.

Bessa now began to show how much he disrelished the idea of my passing through his country, and carrying so much money "behind him," as he expressed it. He offered me his fat bullocks, country cloths, palm-oil, ivory, etc.; but I steadily refused to trade. Finding me inexorable in that respect, he began to grumble about the "dash," or gifts, I had made him. Some mischievous persons had told him that the gifts were insignificant to what it was the custom of Liberians to "dash," or present, kings; and Jollah, my interpreter, had some difficulty to persuade the king to the contrary; besides, he had his own reasons for remaining so incredulous.

I had now struck the line of obstruction at this point. It was upon my refusal to go to Boporu that Kaifal had sent me to Bessa's town. Bessa, in carrying out this policy of non-intercourse with the interior, which is a standing, well-known, and agreed-upon thing throughout the whole country, now commenced a series of annoyances, his people acting in concert with him. He began with my Congoes. Every means that language and signs could produce was used to frighten and discourage them. They were told of the wars in the path. He also showed some Boozies whom he had in his town, whose faces were disfigured with hideous tattoo-marks, and whose front teeth were filed sharp and pointed, for the purpose of eating people; their long bows and poisoned arrows; their broad knives and crooked iron hooks, with which they caught and hewed to pieces those whom they pursued. But what more alarmed my Congoes than any thing else, was the prospect of being eaten by the Boozies. Bessa, to make this part more vividly horrible, had brought into our presence several of his man-eaters, who were said to delight in that business. He then brought in his war-drums, the heads of which were the skins of human beings, well tanned and corded down, while a dozen grinning human jaw-bones were dangling and rattling against each other with a noise that reminded my Congoes that their jaw-bones too might perform a similar office on some country war-drum. It was by such means that Bessa entirely succeeded in disorganizing the whole expedition. He gave the Congoes plainly to understand that they had better not hazard their lives in attempting to follow me to Musardu.

My carriers, who had hitherto shown willingness and obedience, now began openly to disobey my orders; and my difficulty was greatly increased from the fact that I had not been able to get a single civilized person to accompany me. I had no one, in consequence, to confer with, or to assist me in watching the movements of my mutinous Congoes. It soon became evident that there was an understanding between my Congoes and Bessa, and that all hands were conspiring together against me. Several times I had detected Bessa and the Congoes in secret consultation. I guessed at once the villainy hatching. I tried every means to induce the Congoes to disregard the idle tales that were told them by Bessa and his people; but neither advice, persuasion, nor the offer of donations above their pay could overcome the impression that had been made upon their minds respecting the dangers of the route. Big Ben, the Krooman, kept himself aloof from the plots of the Congoes, yet he was in favor of returning to Monrovia; and he made my ears ring with, "'Spose we no find good path; we go back now." The Congoes began to hold secret meetings by themselves, and to talk in a low, muttering tone. Matters were now brewing to some mischievous point; but what their resolves were, I could never learn. With my Congoes in open rupture, Bessa himself drunk, avaricious, and conspiring, I had now to exercise the greatest vigilance.

One night, exasperated at their mutinous language and conduct, we came to a collision, in which all of us had recourse to our arms, and but for the immediate interference of the town people, things would have certainly ended seriously. I should have been riddled with their balls, there being fifteen of them. King Bessa, attended by some of his people, came to allay the disturbance. He could not have been furnished with a better opportunity of seemingly protecting me from the very mischiefs he had secretly instigated. He reproved the Congoes, and imposed a fine for breaking the peace—a gun and a piece of handkerchief being the cost of court. He never used his authority to enforce obedience on the part of the Congoes, which he could have easily done. No; he affected a neutral course, which had many by-paths to his own interest, and through which he managed to transfer many a bar of my tobacco into his own hands.

Much of Bessa's conduct arose from the defiant and refractory behavior of Prince Manna toward the government. The moral effect of this man's conduct has been any thing but beneficial for Liberia. Bessa was continually referring, with pride, to a man who could defy the government with impunity. Unless the government shows energy and control, it will always be difficult to visit these parts—almost within the territorial limits of Liberia—for any purpose whatever. The fact was but too plainly humiliating, that we had lost *prestige* and respect. The policy of too much moderation and forbearance is often abused or misunderstood by warlike barbarians, whose swords are an appendage of their daily apparel.

Bessa now, in an advisory manner, repeated over and over again the difficulties of the route, adding to it the determination of my Congo carriers themselves not to go any further. To this he joined a series of petty annoyances — sometimes coming himself, and sometimes sending for me, to talk palavers. Then he would complain that the Congoes endangered the lives of his people by their hunting; that they would likely set his town on fire by their smoking-pipe, though his own people indulged in this thing not only to a greater degree, but solely through my liberality. But what exasperated me most was his practice of eavesdropping; his boys and people were continually lurking to hear what was said in my house. I was always expected to conclude his royal visits—which were frequent, and which he gave me to understand were condescensions on his part—with large bars of my tobacco.

Bessa is naturally avaricious. This vice was unfortunately worked up to its worst resource; he drank night and day, until he had sufficiently steamed himself up to the courage for downright robbery. Drunk he gets every day; and after the first two or three hours of excess are over, he finally sobers down to that degree at which his avarice is greatest, and his regard for other people's rights least. There he remains.

His couch, upon which he reclines, and which is at once his bed and his chair of state, he never quits, but for a drunken carousal in the midst of his women. This bed is stacked head and foot with loaded muskets, huge horse-pistols, rusty swords and spears, while sundry daggers, with their points stuck in the ground, are ready at hand "for the occasion sudden." He seems to live in perpetual dread of assassination. His people never come in his presence but in an obsequious stoop, and they never recover an erect posture until they are out of his presence. But when the women came, then you might expect to see humanity go on all fours. It was difficult to know the height of some of the women on account of this servility.

Bessa is engaged in the slave-trade. Passing one morning through his town, I saw a slave with his right hand tied up to his neck, and fifty sticks of salt fastened to his back, about to be sent into the interior to be exchanged for a bullock. Six slaves, chained together, worked on his farms. He has numerous other slaves, but they were better treated.

I will not relate all the circumstances of his lashing

an old slave until his cries drew the tears of all who stood by, nor his stamping in the breast of one of his slaves until death ensued, on account of some slight offense. His enormities are too many to recount them all, and would only weary the reader with what they know must be his habits, from what I have already said of him. He regretted to me the interference of the Liberians with the foreign slave-trade.

It was now the beginning of April, and I had not been able to proceed upon my journey. My Congo carriers refused to go any further. Kaifal, the Mandingo, still remained at Vannswah. I therefore tried to induce Bessa to hire me some of his people. I offered to pay him liberally if he would honestly engage in sending me forward. He accepted the offer, and received an amount of $66.40 in goods. He gave me four persons, to act as interpreters and guides; but I had no one to carry my luggage, and he took good care that no one should be hired for that purpose. He was continually telling me that my money "no got feet this time."

If I could have relied on my Congoes, I would have gone on, despite Bessa's attempts to prevent me; but their defection paralyzed all movement forward. I could bethink myself of no other resource than to return to Vannswah in quest of Kaifal. Not having any one in whom I could repose confidence enough to place my effects in their care until I returned from Vannswah, I had to run the risk of placing them in the hands of the king. On the 5th of April, 1868, taking two of my Congoes with me, I came to Boporu. There I met Seymoru Syyo, Kaifal's relation, a tall, fine-looking

Mandingo, but whose very black countenance wore a still blacker cloud of displeasure because I had not come to him direct, instead of going to Bessa. He scarcely deigned to look at me, especially as I was in no decent plight, having undertaken the journey barefoot, in order to cross the streams more readily. He at length gave me to understand that, so far as Kaifal's going to Musardu was concerned, it depended entirely upon his (Seymoru Syyo's) pleasure; muttered something about the war at Musardu; counted his beads, and then strode off toward the mosque, where they had just been summoned to prayer.

On the 6th of April, 1868, I started from Boporu, and arrived at Vannswah on the 9th. Kaifal affected regret at having caused me so much delay, telling me that it was owing to his preparation to get ready that he was detained so long. He now promised to march immediately. This he made a show of doing by sending his women and scholars forward, telling me to go on with them, while he should remain behind to pray for our success. I consented; but he managed to lag behind so long, that I never saw him again until May 8th, after I had left Bessa's and come to Boporu.

I now went back to Bessa's town, persuaded that Kaifal would soon follow. As soon as I arrived at Bessa's, Ben, the Krooman, informed me that the Congoes had tried to induce the king to send them home, telling him that he might keep all my goods if he would only permit them to go home. I went straight to the king, and requested him to deliver to me my boxes; he at once hesitated, and I could scarcely get him to consent to let me have the box containing my clothes. After much contention and wrangling, he delivered up all the boxes, retaining the powder and guns. He then declared that I must pay him for all the Congoes I had placed in his hands; that I must pay him a piece of cloth and a gun for each one of them, as well as for feeding them while I was gone to Vannswah. He then made some other frivolous demands, which he deemed necessary to justify the robbery he was about to commit.

To make the matter worse, the Congoes themselves now began to gather round me like little children, begging me to sacrifice all my goods, if it were necessary, to save them. "Daddy, no lose we this country, no lose we," was their continual whine. All spirit for a manly resistance had fled; nothing but the most abject cowardice prevailed. Before I started on the journey, I had thoroughly armed these Congoes; but the only use they had made of their arms was to resist my authority. Now a peculiar danger stared them in the face—they had not even courage enough to save themselves from slavery.

I refused to comply with the demands of the king to pay the boys. I became exasperated; but I was jammed between the power of the king and the cowardice and unfaithfulness of the Congoes. The king's Boozies, who walked the town with their broad knives to fight, and their teeth filed sharp to eat their enemies, confirmed the poltroonery of the Congoes as a standing and immutable fact.

The king advised the Congoes to talk to me, telling them, "Your daddy has got the heart of an elephant; you had better talk to him." They attempted to talk to me; but I was too much angered at their cowardice and his robbery to listen to any thing. The king extorted $130; Ben, the Krooman, and Louis, a Congo, negotiating the business. I refused to have any thing to do with it. After he had taken this amount, Ben and Louis begged him to be satisfied. He told them that he would refer the matter to his women; if they consented, he would rest satisfied. This female assembly was consulted, and from the subsequent conduct of the king, they must have resolved that I should pay doubly. The extortions were renewed to an amount of $25. This occurred on Friday and Saturday, the 23d and 24th of April.

The next day I was somewhat able to command my feelings. I resolved to go to Boporu. Nothing was more contrary to Bessa's wishes. He now tried his best to induce me to go on my journey through his country. He declared that unless the Congoes wanted to lose their heads, they should go along with me. He was willing to furnish guides and interpreters. But my resolution was taken; I was determined to go to Boporu; no blandishments nor hollow professions of friendship could lead me to trust him after what I had just experienced at his hands. As he had been visited by some suspicious persons, who even counted the number of my Congo warriors, it might have been agreed on to finish with murder what had been begun by robbery. We were allowed to depart without further annoyance. The Congoes were overjoyed; for they were sure that I was returning home. Bessa even sent six stalwart slaves to carry me, in order that my feelings might be soothed into some kind of forbearance toward him; for he now began to fear that I might bring him to account, though it seemed he was willing to run the risk rather than restore the goods. I availed myself of the service of his carriers; but I left the king with the bitter intention to do him all the injury I could as soon as opportunity presented itself.

I arrived at Boporu on the 25th of April, 1868. Kaifal had not yet come, and did not arrive until three days afterward. He now appeared indignant at Bessa's conduct, and affected the greatest diligence for our setting out immediately for Musardu. But first, he would go to Bessa and influence him to restore what he had unjustly taken from me. He induced me to make considerable presents to his friend and relation, Seymoru Syyo, helping himself also in a manner which nothing but my great anxiety for him to hasten our journey would have allowed me to permit.

Before he went to Bessa's, the principal Mandingoes in the town, Kaifal, and myself, held a council, in which they strove to induce me to return to Bessa's with Kaifal; but I utterly refused. I would talk of nothing but soldiers, cannon, the burning of Bessa's town, and other furious things; which so alarmed the Mandingoes, that they begged me not to write to Monrovia about the matter until Kaifal had gone and tried to get the money. In this council, the Mandingoes reminded me that, as the Liberians and Mandingoes were one and the same people, I ought not to act with too great a severity; but I was not inclined to make common stock of my goods on account of that identity, and in a very impatient and unreasonable manner I gave them to understand that all their relationship to me depended solely on the restoration of my goods. If they failed in that, I was prepared to ignore all ties. I was in no humor for cant about kindred; I wanted my money; my feelings were sore at my disappointments and losses.

The expedition was deemed to have fallen in pieces. My interpreter, Jollah, also commenced to show signs of desertion and treachery. I had always suspected him with being implicated in Bessa's villainy; I was soon to discover that he had not been entirely ignorant nor innocent with respect to Bessa's designs. His connivance, or rather the assistance he gave Bessa, was so glaring, that the Mandingoes at Boporu did not fail to upbraid him with it. In his conversation, he plainly showed that he had gone over to Bessa's interest, though he still continued to follow my boxes. The Mandingoes contemptuously asked him in whose service he was, whether mine or Bessa's? Bessa, it seemed, had promised him largely if he (Jollah) assisted him successfully in his villainy. Jollah's crooked ways were such that I could no longer retain his services. Interpreters began to prove a dangerous attachment to the expedition. Owing to Jollah's double-dealing, I was obliged to have recourse to a Veyman to act as interpreter; and right in the middle of an important conversation which I was holding with Seymoru Syyo, this man suffered himself to be taken so ill as to become speechless, and he could only be induced to recover by the promise of a large (dash) present.

Kaifal, it seemed, had greatly offended Seymoru Syyo by sending me to Bessa's instead of sending me direct to Boporu; but, as I have before shown, it was not Kaifal's fault that I did not go directly to Boporu. However, the fault was imputed to him, and as he could only regain the favor of Seymoru by gifts, it was thought no more than right that I should bestow them, as it was through my persistence in refusing to go to Boporu that he had got into the difficulty with Seymoru. As soon as my boxes arrived at Boporu, Seymoru altered his demeanor toward me. His dark and grumbling countenance immediately changed into a smiling intimacy and friendship. He would fain have posted me on wings to Musardu.

Though Boporu is the capital of the Boatswain or Condo country, and the usual residence of the king, Momoru Son, the king was at this time residing at a large town called Totoquella, eight miles north-east of Boporu.

As soon as Kaifal started for Bessa's town, I resolved to pay my respects to King Momoru. I arrived at Totoquella on May 7th, 1868. I was kindly received, and at once stated to the king that I would have been to see him much sooner, but that I was a stranger in his country, and had supposed that he resided at his reputed capital, Boporu; that when I came to that town, I was informed that he had gone elsewhere. He replied that he was accustomed to divide his time between the two towns; sometimes residing at Boporu and sometimes staying at Totoquella. I then informed him of the object of my visit; and had to frame such an account of my former proceedings as to show that it had always been my intention to come to his country, but that I had been thwarted by many untoward circumstances. And true it was that I would have preferred, at the first, going direct to Boporu, had it not been for the reasons already stated.

Circumstances now forced me in that direction, and I addressed myself to the task of repairing the failures or misfortunes into which the expedition had fallen. The king was intelligent and communicative. He was, however, chagrined that the government—the new administration of which had just come into power—had not taken any notice of him, and sent him a (book) paper, expressive of its good feelings toward him, as had been the custom of all incoming administrations. He was always referring to a treaty that had been made between him and President Benson, during the incumbency of the latter. I had, therefore, to console him with the notion that, as soon as the administration had got fairly into operation, it would not fail to draw up an instrument similar to what President Benson had given him; as well as to make such other arrangement as would satisfy his utmost wishes. The king informed me that he was at that moment trying to stop a war between the Boozies and Barlines, two interior tribes; that he had, in order to promote that purpose, sent five hundred sticks of salt into the Barline country, and the same amount to the Boozies; that he had instructed his messengers to use every argument to incline the parties to peace; that the war was not only hurtful to themselves, but that it damaged him by interrupting all intercourse between his country and theirs, and even with the natives whose country lay behind them. He had sent, therefore, to beg both parties to desist; but if neither would listen, he intended to indemnify himself for such losses as he sustained by their feuds, by seizing persons and property belonging to them in his country. If only one party was willing to comply with his requests, he intended to assist that side with his own military forces.

Thus I had to endure the spectacle of a barbarian king practicing a policy which all intelligent and enterprising persons must think ought to be practiced by the republic itself. No one suspects that we leave to an untutored barbarian the quieting and settling of interior difficulties, while we remain ignorant of their very existence.

Every one would suppose that, to a source to which we look for a great part of our interior trade, such as country cloths, and bullocks, and ivory, a rational solicitude, at least, would be shown that it be not interrupted or broken off. Yet it is a fact that this royal barbarian, without revenue, and without any of the resources to which we pretend, by following the policy of interfering in all interior concerns, is better known and has greater influence from Boporu to Musardu, and even beyond, than the civilized Republic of Liberia; and this is done by sending a few sticks of salt, accompanied by a friendly request or a threatening mandate.

Salt, in the settling of difficulties, has a peculiar propriety—it is a sign of peace as well as a commodity of value for traffic. If it was the policy of the government to interfere in these concerns, a hogshead of salt might pacify the whole country from Boporu to Barline. The king had also interfered in a matter between the Boozies themselves; in which it seemed that one of their chiefs, faithless to the common interest, had clandestinely given assistance to the Barlines against his own countrymen. This treachery being discovered, he had been seized and confined—or put in stick, as they call it. This mode of confinement consists in having the ankle of the right foot bound securely to a heavy log, four or five feet long, by means of an iron band driven deep into the wood.

The father of this recreant chief, before his death, had placed his children under King Momoru's protection. The king was therefore solicitous that this indiscretion should not cost the young prince his liberty, and perhaps his head; of the former of which he had already been deprived, and the latter was being seriously discussed among the Boozie chiefs. In this affair the king desired that, as I would have to pass through that country, he wished me to assist in pleading for the young man. I pledged my best efforts.

There was also a difficulty between the king and the Boondee people, who live north-west of Boporu. These people hold a nominal fealty to King Momoru, and even this they are slack or remiss in acknowledging.

The king now chose to remove his court from Totoquella to Boporu. None was more eager for this change than myself; for it carried his person and influence just where I wished to make use of them. He left the town May 10th, 1868, accompanied by his courtiers, warriors, women, servants, and musicians of the last of which there were two kinds: those who performed on horns and drums, and those who sang the praises of the king, timing their music with a sort of iron cymbal, one part being fitted to the thumb of the left hand, and beaten with a piece of iron by the right.

When the king and his retinue had passed the outer gates of the barricade, a Mandingo priest came out and pronounced a benediction on the royal departure. As soon as this was over, we started; the king walking all the way: he had but to say the word, and they would have carried him. We were preceded by the singing men, who, with the clang of their iron cymbals and their vociferous vocalisms, nearly deafened me. After two or three hours spent in traveling, halting, singing, firing muskets, and all sorts of noisy demonstrations, we came to Boporu. The king entered the town and went directly to his own residence. Every body came to do homage and welcome his arrival. But nothing appeared more respectful than the Mandingo priests, who came in a body, habited in their white and scarlet robes; tall, dignified black men, with countenances solemn and intelligent. It is remarkable how orderly and sociable these gatherings upon such occasions conduct themselves. Nothing of the rowdyism and clamor for which communities highly civilized are sometimes notorious. The day was concluded with dancing, feasting, and warlike exercises. The next day beheld every thing settled down into its usual routine. I was now to discover the character of Kaifal in its true light. He had always affected piety and uprightness; nothing very material had occurred to alter my opinion. To be sure, he had lately shown intense craving for my large silver spoon, yet I was inclined to be charitable to this human weakness. He went to Bessa's, solemnly assuring me that he would be gone but two or three days; he staid three weeks, which caused my patience, and confidence too, to grow less. I dispatched two of my boys after him. Upon the return of my messengers, I was informed that he had been generously entertained by Bessa, that a sheep had been slain, and other good offices done for him. I became alarmed lest such friendly cheer would lessen his zeal to recover my goods. But when I was further informed that Kaifal had been engaged in practicing certain rites, such as the interment of beef-bones bound round with transcripts from the Koran, which was to be efficacious for Bessa in peace or war, I immediately understood this last act to be directed against myself. I therefore lost no time in ingratiating myself with the king. And there was scarcely any thing I had to propose that was not favorably entertained and facilitated. I had strengthened my influence by gifts, as well as by the great amusement my stereoscope afforded him. I had thoroughly instructed him in the purposes of my mission; and showed him how discreditable it would be to his name and his honor if any thing should befall me and my effects within the precincts of his dominions, so that I should not be able to carry out the wishes of the promoters of the expedition. In this part of my affairs I was particularly blessed by Providence in getting in my interest a near relation of the king's. He was a Golah man by the civilized name of Chancelor. He had long resided both at Monrovia and Cape Palmas with one of the best citizens, Dr. S. F. McGill, and could speak English fluently, besides several native tongues. He adhered with unflagging zeal to my interest, and never ceased importuning his royal kinsman night and day respecting my affairs.

He was of mild disposition, full of encouragement and sympathy; having nothing to contradict the universal benevolence of his person and character except a huge, antiquated horse-pistol, without which he was never seen, and which became a subject of merriment, as being a burden without a benefit, perfectly innocent in all things except its weight. I had now determined to use all my influence against Kaifal and Bessa. I had been robbed of one part of my goods by the one, and inveigled out of another part by the other. The purposes of the expedition had been baffled, though I had striven to the utmost to accomplish them.

Momoru might be avaricious, but his avarice was a virtue to Bessa's rapacity and Kaifal's unprincipled dealings. If the king wished me to give him any thing, his requests were always accompanied with politeness and desert, arising from the prospect of his facilitating my journey to Musardu. I made a formal complaint against Kaifal and Bessa; presenting the king a written list of all the goods they had unfairly gotten from me. He convened the leading Mandingoes of the town and the principal chiefs. The king himself opened this grand palaver, declaring "that owing to the acts of some of the Mandingoes, many things had been said by the Liberians tending to lessen his character. Whenever the Liberians lost their money by trade or otherwise, he had always to bear the brunt of their dishonest actions and to suffer all kinds of disparagement of character." Nor did he neglect to cite the instances; mentioning as a particular case that of John B. Jordan, who had traded in that country and lost considerable amounts; and then he went on in detail, until he became angered. The Mandingoes found it necessary to appease him by all sorts of condescension; even the singing men were called in. It was necessary to adjourn, that the royal displeasure might cool off.

The next day the business was resumed. It is the custom for every body taking part in a (palaver) discussion, to deliver his argument or opinion walking up and down in the presence of his audience with a spear in his hands.

This mode was observed by all the chiefs who spoke on this occasion. Many of them delivered themselves with such spirit and sense as to draw the frequent acclamations of their hearers. They declared that they not only ought to be careful about provoking the Americans against them; but, as the money was for the purpose of (dashing) presenting the chiefs through whose country I might pass, I ought to be allowed to give it to whom I wished; and that none ought to accept it unless they were willing to accept the conditions of the gift also.

For the conduct of Bessa and Kaifal, the Mandingoes at Boporu seemed to have been held as sureties; certainly not by their own will or consent, but by virtue of their being most conveniently at hand for any purpose of indemnification that might arise. Kaifal, who was still at Bessa's town, was summoned to appear. Bessa was ordered to refund every article according to the list.

The messenger charged with this business went to Bessa's in the most formal manner, being in complete war-dress. It was, therefore, understood that there was to be no trifling.

Things began now to conspire in my favor.

Just about this time a young man by the name of Sanders Washington, from the settlement of Virginia, went to Bessa's town for the purpose of trading. Here he learned what had happened between Bessa and myself. He at once advised Bessa to restore the money before the consequences became serious. Bessa, becoming more sober than was usual with him, commenced to apprehend a severe chastising from the government, and right upon the heels of what was to be feared from the Americans came Momoru's no less dreaded demands.

Bessa quickly gave up the things to Mr. Sanders Washington, and consoled himself in a drunken spree. Mr. Washington immediately sent the things to Boporu.

Kaifal now made his appearance. It was the 28th of May, 1868. He came before the king and council dressed in a dark-blue tobe; a red cap bordered with a white band, the badge of his sacerdotal order, on his head; sandals on his feet; his prayer-beads in his hands; his face and faculties prepared for the worst. He was ordered to account for the manner he had conducted my affairs. He commenced defending himself by declaring that what had happened to me was the result of my own obstinacy; for when he wished to send me directly to Boporu, I had insisted on going elsewhere. He further said that if I could have passed through the country anywhere else, they would have never seen my face at Boporu; which was indeed true. He caused disagreeable questions to be put to me respecting that matter: this was his only advantage, and he clung to it. He declared that I had absolutely refused to go to Boporu, and that I had maligned the king, and that I had gone to Bessa's, where my indiscretion had got me into trouble and made me lose my money; that Bessa had acted in all things honestly.

His argument was partly true and partly false. All he averred respecting Boporu was indeed true; but borrowing the courage which the truth about Boporu gave him, his assertions about Bessa's conduct were bold and barefaced lies. I replied that it was solely upon his advice that I had gone to Bessa's; that as to my coming to Boporu, he plainly saw I was there, and that without consulting him.

He dwelt incessantly on my refusal to go to Boporu, and more than once it was convenient for me to rid myself of his vexing questions by placing the whole blame upon his interpreter.

We now came to that part in which he had taken my money and gone off to Bessa's, where he had staid so long that it became necessary to send for him. Being questioned why he had done so, his self-possession entirely forsook him, and though he referred the matter to a rapid manipulation of his beads, it brought him no relief. He told them over and over, but they failed to enlighten his mind so as to furnish prompt replies and ready answers. He finally stammered out something about his waiting for the new moon. He had not regarded that luminary when he was getting the goods.

He was made to restore according to the list.

I was now in possession of all my goods again, with the prospect of being able to prosecute the exploration with success.

I was also in a better state of mind to attend to my affairs in that respect, though, as I had all along apprehended, the season for comfortable traveling, and especially for making astronomical observations, had nearly passed; indeed, upon every attempt at an observation, clouds and vapor made it a difficult and uncertain matter.

Boporu, the capital of the Boatswain country, is in latitude 7° 45 03″. Its elevation above the level of the sea is about 560 feet. The barometer, in the month of May and June, stands from 29.18 to 29.40; the thermometer ranges from 78 to 80 Fahrenheit. It is situated in a small plain near the foot of some high hills E. N.E. of it. Very high hills rise on every side, with an elevation from 300 to 650 feet, coursing along in every direction, some continuing three or four miles in length before their spurs come down into the valleys or plains. The soil of the plains is chiefly white and yellow clay; but near the base of the hills, it is generally mixed with the detritus of granite and other rocks washed down in the rainy season from their sides. Granite boulders of various sizes are found on the sides and tops of these hills, and, unlike the granite of our cape, which is of a fine, dark flinty appearance, present many grades of tint and texture. A large piece of this granitic gneiss forms a part of the grave of King Boatswain, the present king's father, broken in such a way as to show the red, white, and gray in beautiful contrast. A little art might have rendered it more worthy to mark so mighty a grave. Every tree, flower, and shrub of our cape repeats itself here, not excepting the water-lilies seen in the creeks as you go to Junk, though not in the same profusion.

At Totoquella, north-east of Boporu, and four hours' walk south-east from the former, the St. Paul's River presents rugged and impassable falls. North-west of Totoquella are beds of specular iron-ore, which the natives break into fragments and use for shot.

The population of Boporu is of a mixed character, such as war, commerce, and the domestic slave-trade are calculated to produce; in consequence of which there are as many different languages spoken as there are tribes: Vey, Golah, Mambomah, Mandingo, Pessy, Boozie, Boondee, and the Hurrah languages. The Vey language is used for general communication. The extent and population of these tribes are very variable elements. The population living in the town may be set down at three thousand; but then there are many outlying villages and hamlets; and considering these as the suburbs of Boporu, they undoubtedly raise the population to ten thousand. Many of the Mandingoes themselves, though they reside in the town with their families, have villages of slaves and servants scattered in every direction, wherever the purposes of agriculture invite or encourage.

The Mandingoes possess strong moral influence. Scarcely any thing is undertaken without consulting their priests, whose prayers, blessings, and other rites are supposed to give a propitious turn to all the affairs of peace and war. They are Mohammedans; but as the ruder tribes do not addict themselves to the intellectual habits of the Mandingoes, it has been found necessary to adjust that faith to the necessities of the case; and to temper some of the mummeries of fetichism with the teachings of Islam. Yet are there to be found individuals who do not prostitute their faith, and who are more scrupulous and sincere. It is believed by many persons that the Arabic learning of our Mandingoes, in reading and writing from the Koran, is merely mechanical, or a mere matter of memory.

Kaifal took a small Arabic grammar given to me by Professor Blyden, and showed himself thoroughly versed in all the distinctions of person, gender, and number, etc., in the conjugation of a verb. However, all are not equally proficient in this respect.

They have a mosque at Boporu, where nothing enjoined by their religion is omitted. It is attended solely by the Mandingoes, none of the other tribes visiting it; not because they are prohibited, for the Mandingoes would make proselytes of them all if they could. It is sufficient for the "Kaffirs," (unbelievers,) as they are denominated by the Mandingoes, to buy the amulets, necklaces, and belts containing transcripts from the Koran sewed up in them, to be worn around the neck, arms, or waist as preservatives from the casualties of war, sickness, or ill luck in trade or love.

The Mandingoes are scrupulously attentive to their worship. They regularly attend their services three times a day: five o'clock in the morning; three o'clock in the afternoon; and seven o'clock in the evening.

In these services I was particularly attracted by the manner in which they chanted the cardinal article of their creed; and many a morning have I been reminded of my own duty, by their solemn musical voices reciting:

La il-la-ha il-al-la hu Ma-hamma-du ra-sul il-la-hi.

The Mandingoes living in the Boatswain country have many slaves. The slave population is supposed to treble the number of free persons. They are purchased chiefly from the Pessy, Boozie, and other tribes. Many are reduced to the condition of slaves, by being captured in war. Their chief labor is to perform the service of carriers for their masters in the trade of salt and country cloths carried between Boporu and Vannswah.

Inconveniences and troubles frequently arise from this kind of relationship. Sensible of their numbers and strength, the slaves sometimes make a struggle for their liberty. In the latter part of 1866, at the death of Torsu, King Momoru's uncle, it became necessary to settle some debts pertaining to Torsu's estate. His relatives, in order to pay off the claims, attempted to sell some of his slaves. These slaves were staying at a town called Musadalla's town, south-west of Boporu. The attempt was resisted; some blood was shed; and a general revolt took place, in which all the slaves in the town determined to defend each other to the last extremity. They took full possession of the town, renewed the barricades, seized upon whatever arms were at hand, and made such other preparations as greatly alarmed their masters. This rebellion had been long purposed on; the death of Torsu and the attempt to sell some of their number, served as a favorable opportunity to achieve their freedom.

On the first outbreak, King Momoru sent them word

to return to their former obedience, assuring them that he would overlook all past offenses. But while they were deliberating as to what answer they should return, one of their women publicly harangued them against listening to any proposals for reconciliation; that King Momoru only wished to induce them to submit, that he might the more easily punish them; that if their hearts began to quail, they had better give their spears into the hands of the women.

This speech instantly determined them to stand fast in their first resolutions. Refusing all accommodation, they sought to strengthen their cause by purchasing the assistance of the Boondee people, who were at that time at variance with the people at Boporu. But the Boporu people had also managed, despite their difference with the Boondee people, to engage their services against the slaves. The Boondee war chief received the gifts of both parties; and in two weeks' time repaid the poor slaves with treachery enough to chop off their heads.

Arming himself and his people, he set out for Musadalla's town, and was admitted by his unsuspecting victims. After he had rested from his journey, and refreshed himself and his followers on their generosity, he proposed to review their numbers and their arms. Pretending to be earnestly enlisted in their affairs, he bade them lay their arms on the ground, or, as we term it, "ground arms," that he might the better judge of their efficiency. The poor, credulous fools, by no means suspecting any perfidy, readily did as they were bid. At a given signal from the Boondee chief, his own people instantly drew their swords and bestrode the weapons of the poor slaves as they lay on the ground. Thus disarmed, they were thus again enslaved, seized, bound, and led out of the gates to the town of their betrayer, who at once sent word to Momoru that he had caught the "slave dogs." He was rewarded, or rather he rewarded himself, by keeping all the women and children, sending to Momoru only the men and our heroine who, by her speech, had so greatly encouraged the matter. It was determined in council that the slaves should suffer the penalty of death.

On the morning of the execution they were demanded to say who were the chief instigators of the revolt; the poor creatures had but little to say. They were led out of the eastern gate, two hundred yards from which, and in the same direction, stands a huge cotton-tree (bombax)—the place of execution. They came down the path naked, and in single file, with their hands bound behind them. As the first person came on, the executioner with his broad and gleaming knife ran to meet him, and with dexterous cruelty emasculated him; after allowing him to bleed and beg awhile, he was snatched down to the foot of the tree, his head hacked off and tossed into a ditch on one side of the road; while the yet quivering trunk was thrown into a cat-fish pond hard by.

The woman was executed with circumstances shocking to humanity and decency. All the women in Boporu were compelled to go out and witness her fate.

But to the chief of this revolt it was reserved to be buried alive, heels up and head down, and a sharp stake, eight feet long, driven through his body level with the ground, and a tree planted over him. Their skulls now form a ghastly adornment to the eastern gate; and I have seen many persons go up to them and recognize an acquaintance.

It seems to be the practice in every town where the water favors it to have cat-fish pools. The fish are not allowed to be disturbed; they are not only the consumers of the offal of the town, but from their shark-like and snappish manner, a more fearful office can well be suspected. They are from one to three feet long, and will lie with patience and expectation in one spot all day long, their backs raw with scars, which their own ferocity inflicts on each other in the fierce struggle for food.

Boporu has a small market, held in the north-east suburbs of the town. The bartering is carried on solely by women. There is no established currency; the exchange takes place of one commodity for another, according to their mutual necessities. It is generally attended by one hundred and seventy-five to two hundred persons. The articles are palm-oil, rice, kaffee-seed, shallots—a small species of onion—meat, cotton stripes, tobacco, kola, earthen pots, etc. A great many country cloths are made at Boporu, every family having a small loom. They would economize both time and labor if they would employ our large loom, instead of the narrow six-inch loom they use. I have no doubt they would do so, if any civilized person would interest himself to show them.

These people are very sensible of the superiority of every thing that comes from (Dru-kau) Monrovia, and they attempt to practice our civilization of themselves.

The king has a frame house at Totoquella, with a piazza surrounding it, all of native construction. He also uses chairs, tables, beds, bedsteads, looking-glasses, scented soaps, colognes, etc. He took great interest in examining my sextant, and even the pictures in my books; but that which afforded him the greatest pleasure was the stereoscope. He entreated me so earnestly to leave it with him, that I felt myself bound to gratify his wishes in that respect, though I had specially intended it for Musardu.

He was no less satisfied when I flattered him with the prospect of a school for children being established at Boporu, telling me that when John B. Jordan traded there, he was accustomed to get Jordan to teach him.

The king spells a little, and is somewhat acquainted with numbers. This is the place for the missionary to be of service; but it seems that, though Mohammed has a small mosque and school at Vannswah, almost in the Virginia settlement, the Christians have neither church nor school at Boporu.

The king's authority seems to be of a mixed character. In some things he acts absolutely; while in others, such as war, he takes the counsel of the subordinate chiefs. He is judge or arbiter of all important differences between his subjects. He is a most patient hearer of all matters brought before him. I have known him to remain in his hammock for whole days, listening to what was to be said by either side, and his decisions seemed to be generally satisfactory.

A very peculiar but advantageous method obtains in the administration of justice. In order to obviate all further trouble after the decision is given, both plaintiff and defendant have to advance the cost and expenses before the suit begins; the very articles in which these charges are to be paid are placed in a conspicuous manner in the sight of every body. The presence of the money thereby becomes an incentive and stimulation to strenuous effort. As soon as the case is decided, nothing remains but for the victor to sweep the stakes. These cases between his subjects are frequently taxing and vexatious, yet the king is said to always preside with patience and a well-balanced impartiality.

But the king sometimes takes recreation from the severe affairs of life, at which time he is apt to enliven the hours of vacation from business with a glass of gin or whisky, and then he goes playfully around the town attended by his people. It happens that his caprice is as innocent then as his gentle disposition is in his sober hours; for he hurts no one; only going from house to house, joking with and receiving little presents from his friends. Sometimes he attempts to dance, or to act some warlike feat; but want of youth and a rather fat body mar the practice. One day he insisted on the performance, to his no small discomfiture. He mounted himself upon an earthen hill, with a spear in each hand, in order to charge down in warlike style; starting in full tilt, he came sprawling to the ground with such violence as to scarify the royal bosom in a most unseemly manner.

Before I left Boporu for the interior, the king informed me that the distance, danger, and hazard were so great, that he must consult the sand-doctor as to the final issues of such a journey. He declared that, upon all such important matters, he trusted not to human prudence alone. This individual, the sand-doctor, by giving his fingers certain motions in a small pile of sand, is supposed to read the events of the future. We were carried into a thatch hut. Our diviner, spreading out a small pile of sand with his right hand, began to invoke the demon of the pile. The whole thing was conducted without thunder, lightning, or any thing else, except the rapid, voluble utterances of our diviner himself. Again and again it was demanded of the flinty wisdoms whether or not the expedition should be successful; the responses indicated by these sandy hieroglyphics bid us begone and prosper. Thus it was that superstition at this time seconded the purposes of a rational inquiry. The king not unfrequently chided me because I was indifferent and incredulous about such matters.

Every effort was made by the Boporu Mandingoes to prevent my going. It was told to Momoru that if any thing befell me, he alone would be held responsible to the government. Even old Gatumba sent word to Momoru not to allow me, under any circumstances whatever, to pass and "go behind them;" for he declared that I was going for no other purpose but to ruin their trade. It was the first time, I was informed, that the king had set himself in opposition to the advice and counsel of his chiefs, many of whom were greatly opposed to my passing through their country to go in the interior. I therefore exerted the greatest industry in purchasing their silence or assistance. But to the Boporu Mandingoes I held threatening language, in which I informed them that if I did not succeed in going to their country, I would return and break up all their trade at Vannswah.

Mr. Schieffelin's money, however, was the most powerful argument. It prevailed over every obstacle; it reconciled me to prejudices and persons the most difficult to deal with; invoked the blessings of Mohammed on my head; caused even the sands to become things of sense in my favor; singularly enlightened minds that before could not see why I wished to go in the interior, and finally reduced the prospect of my going in the interior to the most undoubted moral certainty.

On the 14th of June, I left Boporu for Totoquella; and on June 16th, we left Totoquella for the interior, our company consisting of three Congoes—Jim, Alex, and Pickaninny—as carriers; Chancellor, the Golah, as interpreter, and Beah, the Mandingo, as guide. The rest of my Congoes, numbering fifteen, had returned to Monrovia, giving all kinds of false accounts of our proceedings.

I had now again to experience the effects of the jealousy of the Mandingoes. They had determined that I should not reach Musardu. They therefore gave secret instructions to the Mandingo guide, Beah, who was to accompany me, to delay and shuffle all along the route, so as to exhaust my means and discourage my perseverance, and thus to finally thwart the expedition. It was through this man's tricks that I was compelled to spend six months in going to Musardu, when only one was necessary.

On Tuesday, the 16th of June, we left Totoquella for the interior, the direction being, with very little deviation, east. The hilly features of the country became more striking; large granite boulders were scattered here and there; small creeks, flowing over beds of sand and gravel, drained the country from every direction into the St. Paul's River. About half-past four o'clock P.M., we reached the north-western edge of the Pessy country, and halted at a small hamlet for the night. Here the barometer stood 29.19; thermometer, 84°.

Wednesday, the 17th of June, six A.M., barometer, 29.20; thermometer, 78° Fahrenheit. We pushed on, and passed through another Pessy village. The Pessys seem to have an abundance of poultry, sheep, and rice; here we halted.

Thursday, the 18th of June, we started on our journey, the country bearing the same hilly appearance. We halted at a considerable village, called Sellayo, about twelve o'clock. The chief was swinging in his hammock in a half-finished shed; he was sullen, and scarcely spoke; he, however, deigned to give us a little palm-wine. We made him a small (dash) present, at which he was quite displeased; but we cut short all grumbling by starting off soon in the morning.

Friday, the 19th, we passed through Nesebeah (red hill) and Pollamah, Pessy villages, and halted at Zelleki's town at half-past three P.M. This village contained 250 houses, built in the usual style; the body being of clay and of a circular shape, with thatched conical coverings. This village wore an indifferent appearance, showing scarcely any activity in any species of industry. On account of its sameness, we were glad enough to leave it. Outside of its barricade was a large creek containing cat-fish, as at Boporu.

The only thing that rendered the idle hours tolerable was King Momoru's daughter, who had married a Mandingo residing in the village. She very much resembled her father, and was of the same jovial disposition; and when I left the village, she marched out before me, with my musket at shoulder-arms, at a military pace, imitating what she had seen at Monrovia the last time she was down there with her father.

Saturday, June 20th, 1868, we reached Barkomah, the largest Pessy town in this direction. King Pato is not stamped by nature for a king, and his town is neither commendable for cleanliness nor industry. It contains 300 dilapidated houses, half a dozen cows, some large Mandingo dogs, about 800 inhabitants, and is surrounded on all sides by impenetrable jungle, which is considered a sufficient barrier from all attacks. It is difficult to conceive whether this plan of defense was suggested by cowardice or laziness. We were lodged in a miserable little hut, about twelve feet long by eight feet wide, and five feet high. We had to endure this bamboo cage for ten days, because our guide had friends, who made him as comfortable as we were wretched. We were delayed under various pretexts, the chief of which was that, as my boys had almost given out, assistance had to be procured for carrying our luggage.

On the 1st of July, we started from Barkomah, and crossed a considerable tributary of the St. Paul's River, seventy-five feet wide, running in the direction of south-west between banks of clay, eight feet on one side and fifteen feet on the other, with a velocity of forty feet in fifteen seconds. The stream is ten feet deep in this place, and is known to overflow its banks on the eight-foot side in the depths of the rains. It is crossed on slender poles tied together. Only one person can cross at a time; and just as the burdened traveler reaches the middle, he is arrested by a ticklish swaying that threatens to unbalance him into the waters below; here he dares not move until the restive poles regain their quiet. It has blighted many a prospect, or rather melted many a basket of salt. In days gone by, it was crossed by a suspension-bridge of wicker work, elevated fifteen feet above the surface, as appeared by the remains of logs and withes. This stream separates the Pessy country at this point from the Deh country.

The Deh people are a small tribe intervening between the Pessy and Bonsie people. They seem to be a distinct people, and speak a strong, rough, guttural language, similar to our Kroo tribe on the coast, whom they resemble in many other particulars. They have more fire in their eyes than the Pessy people, and are said to eat their enemies in war. After a half-hour's walk, we passed through the Dey villages of Muc Zuc and Yalah, and halted at Dallazeah. The Deh people, in proffering their hospitalities, offered us dog for dinner, which was politely declined.

On Thursday, the 2d of July, we started from Dallazeah. Farms of rice, corn, cotton, and tobacco succeeded each other in an order truly pleasing to look at. The people are very industrious. The women, on seeing me, began to tremble with fear; and though some of my people, with whom they were well acquainted, tried to assure them, they could not be persuaded to approach me. Keeping the direction east, we passed another Deh village—Malung, (water.) From here we came to the site of a large Deh town—Gellabonda, (lightning)—which had been completely destroyed by a civil war. It was so elevated that we had but to look E. S. E. to see a large part of the Barline country, and the very parts in which war was then raging. Indeed, we had hitherto followed the Barline route; but at two o'clock P.M. our guide, Beah, changed the direction, remarking, as he did so, powder and ball were in the path he had left. We halted at Mahfatah, a small Deh village. At night, one of their houses caught on fire, and but for the activity of our people the whole of their frail bamboo dwellings would have been consumed. These people travel very little, and are consequently ruder, and, as I then supposed, less hospitable than the other tribes. We passed the 4th of July here, the barometer standing at 28.89, thermometer 80°; ten o'clock A.M., weather cloudy.

Friday, the 5th of July, we started on our journey, passing through several Deh villages. We also crossed a small falls called Gawboah, with water rushing over granite beds colored red and gray, with seams of white quartz and red feldspar ramifying the bed in many directions. We halted at Zolaghee, the largest and last town of the Deh people. This town contained 300 houses, more or less in a state of dilapidation. Nothing is more disagreeable than to be obliged to take quarters in these decaying clay-built towns, especially in the rainy season, when the mud, trash, and all the soil, frogs, and vermin of the town dissolve, crumble, and creep too near not to annoy sensibilities accustomed to cleanliness. We managed to tolerate this town one day, in order to rest ourselves.

On the 7th, we reached the Bonsie country, or the Domar division of the Bonsies. We passed through Powlazue, Unzugahzeah, Kaulibodah, and halted at Yahwahzue. These towns are large and densely peopled, surrounded with high and massive walls of clay and earth. It was here that the Barline people had been lately making reprisals, capturing the women and slaves on the farms. It was therefore necessary that our Bonsie friends should exercise constant vigilance, and be ready to sally forth from their walls at a moment's warning to repel these incursions.

You no sooner arrive in the Bonsie country, than a contrast of cleanliness, order, and industry strikes you. That tribe, continually represented to us as savage, fierce, and intractable, at once invites you into its large walled towns with all the hospitalities and courtesy that the minds of this simple, untutored people can think of.

I arrived at Zolu's town on the 8th of July, 1868, at four o'clock P.M. The walls of this town are from eighteen to twenty feet high, consisting of clay, and very thick. A regular salvo of musketry announced my entrance, and quickly a band of music made its appearance, consisting of twelve large and small ivory horns, and a half-dozen drums of various sizes and sounds. I was conducted to the market space, in the centre of the town, and there welcomed amidst the blast and flourish of Bonsie music and the firing of muskets.

They were astonished and overjoyed that (a Weegee) an American should come so far to visit them in their own country. A thousand strange faces, whom I had never before seen, were gazing at me. After their curiosity and wonder had been satisfied, they gave me spacious and comfortable lodgings, and commenced a series of hospitalities which, from mere quantity alone, became oppressive.

The next day, my friends would have me put on American cloth; to please them, I did so. I had not shaved for three months, and when I made my appearance in the 'Merican cloth, together with an unshaven face, the women and children fled in every direction from the frightfully-bearded Weegee. Many a Bonsie child was hushed to silence or sleep by being threatened with the Weegee. I annoyed the women and children at such a rate, that I soon deemed it necessary to take off the American cloth and the beard also.

This part of Africa likes a clean face, and especially a full-flowing gown, which is not only a more graceful attire, but more comfortable and healthy than the tight-fitting pieces which we call civilized clothing. This town, like Boporu, has its small daily market; but the large weekly markêt, which is held every Thursday, and to which the neighboring towns usually resort, is held at Zow-Zow, a very large town fifteen miles E. N. E. of Zolu. I visited this market. The hum of voices could be heard in the distance like the noise of a waterfall. It is attended by five or six thousand people. The bargaining is generally conducted by the women, except the country cloth trade, which is carried on by the men. The exchange is generally a barter—one article is exchanged for another, according to the mutual wants of the buyer and seller. Salt and kola, however, have the character of a currency, and large bargains are generally valued in these articles. They are the expression of prices in all important bargains. Kola usually performs the same service our coppers do in small bargains. These markets also have the character of holiday or pleasure-days. Every one appears in his or her best attire. The women wear blue and colored country cloths girded tastefully around their waists, their heads bound round with a large three-cornered handkerchief of the same material. Blue beads, intermixed with their favorite "pateriki," (brass buttons,) encircle their necks, their faces ornamented with blue pigment and smiles.

In going around the market, and even on the road as you go to the market, you are sure to be loaded with ground-nuts, bananas, and rice-bread. Rice forms the chief breadstuff; cassavas and potatoes next. Potatoes grow to an enormous size, and will weigh from six to eight pounds. My Congo carriers were greatly elated when they bought a bushel of white rice for four brass buttons and a few needles. Considering the large farms and the quantities of old rice from the previous crop which must remain unconsumed, rice can never be a source of profit to these people until they have a road and conveyance to cart it down to some civilized settlement.

The two great farming staples in the Boozie country are rice and cotton. Sometimes the rice and cotton are planted together, but most of the cotton-farms succeed the rice-farms. The cotton-farms bear no proportion in size to the rice-farms, yet they are large; for they have to clothe a country densely populated, where men, women, and children all go clothed, and no foreign manufactures scarcely reach them. Cotton-gins would be a blessing to these people; for the manner in which they are obliged to prepare cotton for spinning is painful and tedious to the last degree of labor. This part of the labor is done by the women; the men do the weaving. The spindle is in the hands of every woman, from the princess to the slave. The dyeing of cloth is also done by the women, at which the Mandingoes are the most expert; and they know how to impart various shades of blue in a permanent and beautiful manner. Though they have abundance of camwood, I have never seen them use it for the purposes of dyeing. The chief colors used are blue and yellow; the latter color is extracted from bark. Taking into account that these people not only clothe themselves, but furnish the vast number of cloths that are brought to the coast to be used in the leeward trade, it shows what the cotton-producing power of the country would become if this primitive, barbarian industry were only assisted by some labor-saving machinery.

On the second day after my arrival, I had a musical compliment paid to me. A dozen young ladies, from ten to eighteen years of age, serenaded me in the following manner: A large mat being spread on the ground before my door, the young ladies seated themselves and commenced singing one of the songs of their country, marking the time, as well as accompanying the music, by means of hollow wooden pipes four and a half inches long, through which the wind is forced by beating one end with the palm of the hand. When this compliment is paid to a friend, one of the young ladies who has tact and talent improvises a solo as to his good qualities, his bravery, his good looks, his generosity, etc., at the conclusion of which all join the chorus, repeating the words, "Emmamow," "Emmamow"—Thank you, thank you. It is also a very delicate way of insinuation, when your liberality does not always satisfy their expectations. My liberality in some cases "becoming small by degrees and beautifully less," a young lady revenged herself on me by singing that I had a " giving face but a stingy heart," at which they all responded, "Kella? Kella?"—Is it so? Is it so? Well, thank you; thank you. This is indeed a very delicate way of insinuation; but the ungenerous little rogue ought to have remembered that it was through my liberality that they were enabled to have all the fine brass buttons which they sported around their necks at the Zow Zow market. However, I hope it will be considered that I have done the state some service, when I announce that I have labeled nearly all the pretty women in the Boozie country as the property of the Republic of Liberia, with its military brass buttons, (pateriki.)

The Boozies are a very polite people; the slightest favor is repaid with an "Emmamow"—Thank you. Do you dance or afford any amusement whatever, you receive the "Emmamow." Are you engaged in any labor or business for yourself or others, you are as heartily " thanked" by those whom it does not in the least concern as if it were for themselves. If you are carrying a heavy burden on the road, and happen to meet a friend, he thanks you as if you were doing it for him. My Congo carriers, who were nearly fagged out with the weight of their burdens, used to be annoyed with this kind of civility, that contained all thanks and no assistance, and the Bonsie "Emmamow" was often exchanged for the Congo "Konapembo," (Go to the devil,) an exhortation not unreasonable where misery is prolonged by politeness, and where one having his back bent, burdened, and almost broke, has to be stopped to be thanked and to snap fingers half a dozen times.

The soil of Zolu is chiefly a red sandstone, and the eastern road, worn down three feet by constant traveling and the successive washings of the rains, exhibits to this depth its internal peculiarities—red sandstone, consolidated in proportion as the depth increases, but of crude and crumbling consistence at the surface, with ramifications of clear and distinct veins of white quartz from one to two and a half inches wide. On some of the hills there are large boulders of granite, and some of them have markings crossing each other nearly in parallels, in a direction from N. W. to S. E. and N. E. to S. W. The markings seem deeply ingrained, and are not so much sensible to the touch as visible to the eye. There is also in this country a stone of a very beautiful green color, capable of receiving a high polish, a large piece of which was placed at the eastern gate of the town for a stepping-stone, and which, in that position, from the frequent treadings it receives, had a finely polished surface. The character of the soil of the plains is principally clay and sand. The red sandstone at Zolu begins in the south-western portion of the Pessy country, at the town called Nessebeah, (red hill;) and it is in this vicinity that the soil, changing from a mixture of clay and sand and granite pebbles, forms a red clayey and sandy composition. Nessebeah is located upon a very elevated hill of red clay and sand, which presents every grade of condensation, from a loose soil to solid rock. In the town were huge granite rocks resting upon elevated beds of this red soil, as if they had been purposely placed there by human effort; but they owe their position to some former power of nature and the subsequent washings of the rains. The elevation and position of these rocks serve to show what vast quantities of soil have been washed down in the plains and valleys below. Very extensive views are had from this site. The sides of the hills being rather steep, the soil, on this account, is inclined to shelve down, and to lay bare entirely its color and composition from the top to the bottom. These red slopes form a curious contrast to the abundant green vegetation with which their summits and the plains below are clothed.

I arrived at Zolu on the 8th of July. Here it was that the Mandingo guide, Beah, according to the instructions that had been given to him by King Momoru, was to spend a couple of weeks in trying to reconcile the differences between the Bonsies and the Barline people. Zolu was also the town belonging to the young chief who had covertly assisted the Barline people, and who was now suffering the penalty of his perfidy. He was confined at Salaghee, a large town fifteen miles east of Zolu, by a chief called Daffahborrah.

Three days after our arrival, Beah went to Salaghee, in order to open negotiations, both for the release of the young prince, Cavvea, and to stop the war between the Bonsies and Barlines. King Momoru had already sent the same proposals for reconciliation to the Barline people by some Mandingoes, who were to act in concert with Beah in bringing about peace. Nor was Daffahborrah disinclined to entertain these proposals for peace. His town being on the confines of the Boozie and Barline territory, was more subject, on this account, to the incursions of the latter, and indeed on his town had fallen most of the brunt of the war.

Beah, after two days' absence at Salaghee, returned. He informed me that Daffahborrah had requested him not to bring me to his town, as he was afraid of the great war-medicine which his people had told him I had in my possession. This war-medicine was a bottle of nitric acid, given me by Dr. Dunbar for the purpose of trying gold. My Congoes having witnessed some of its effects on cloth, metal, etc., had given it a fearful reputation: A table-spoonful scattered in a crowd would kill a hundred men; the least bit on a thatch house would burn up a whole town; I had but to stand outside the walls and throw it in the air to cause destruction to any town. This bottle of "medicine" began to give me great inconvenience; every body refused to carry it. A big bandage of rags and thatch housed the fiery spirit; great was the ceremony in assigning it its place wherever I happened to stop. Daffahborrah could not be blamed for refusing to see me. Beah returned to Salaghee, and remained three weeks.

It was now about the beginning of August, and the depth of the rains; I therefore determined to shun all exposure from the weather. What I particularly dreaded was the losing or damaging my instruments in crossing the creeks, with which a country rugged with every feature of hill and dale is everywhere intersected. In the dries, many of them scarcely contain water enough to cover the foot; but in the rains, they become torrents, eight and ten feet deep, with a swift and destructive current, being, in fact, drains or gullies tilted toward the main reservoirs, the St. Paul's and Little Cape Mount rivers. The rains had fairly set in; yet the quantity of water is much less than what I have been accustomed to experience on the seaboard at Monrovia.

The country is every variety of hill, plain, and valley. Standing upon an elevation, it seemed to me that the people had attempted to cover the whole country with their rice-fields. Toward the west could be seen the rice-hills enveloped in showers; succeeding that, whole mountain-sides of rice partly buried in vapor; next to that could be seen a brilliant sunlight, spread over the brown and ripening plains of rice below.

It would be difficult to describe into how many scenes sunshine, showers, clouds, and vapor can vary a locality, itself an expression of every variety of change. Only here and there could be seen patches of large forest-trees. So completely had this section of the country been farmed over and over, that only saplings of three or four years' growth covered the uncultivated parts. Nor will they be allowed to attain a greater age or size before the requirements of agriculture will clear them for rice and cotton-fields.

This is the chief reason why all the barricades, or walls of towns, in this section of the country, are formed of earth and clay, instead of the large stakes that are used by the natives living in the vicinity of Liberia.

The Bonsie people have very tractable dispositions, and are wedded to no particular species of error. Fetichism has no strong hold on them. They believe in that thing most that manifests the greatest visible superiority or power. They are greatly duped by the fraud and chicanery of the Mohammedan Mandingo priests.

In general physical appearance the Boozies are well built, generally from five and a half to six feet high in stature, with stoutly developed bodies, of sufficient muscular strength to hold a United States musket, bayonet fixed, at full arm's length in one hand. They are an exceedingly healthy people, and of very clean habits. They bathe regularly twice a day, night and morning, in warm water, besides the intermediate cold water baths they are sure to take at whatever creek they happen to cross in their daily walking. For cleaning the teeth, they use a brush made of ratan, admirably adapted to the purpose.

Paring the finger and toe-nails is carried to excess. And the women at Zolu are foolish enough to pluck away part of their eyebrows and eyelashes, things which nature had not too lavishly furnished them from the first.

Many of the women are very pretty; and for the

many faces with which I am acquainted at Monrovia resemblances, and close resemblances, are to be found among the Boozies. Most of our people at Monrovia are fond of deriving themselves from the Mandingoes. I am sorry to say that this Boozie type of resemblance does not confirm an origin so noble and consoling. We must therefore rest satisfied with humbler antecedents.

As soon as the weather permitted traveling, I insisted on Beah resuming the journey. But he framed many excuses, and finally, to rid himself of my importunities, ran off to Bokkasah, where his family resided. Thither I dispatched one of my boys, demanding his return; but he refused to come. Beah was trying to carry out the secret instructions he had received from the Boporu Mandingoes. To trammel and obstruct my going still more, he sent word to the Boozies at Zolu that they were not to allow me to go anywhere; for if any thing befell Momoru's American man, they alone would be held responsible for it. Three times I endeavored to leave this town; but the people, by entreaties, presents, and every means of persuasion they could think of, compelled me to relinquish my intentions.

Beah had duped them as to the real reasons of delay. Finally, it was appointed that if Beah should not return in two weeks, I was to go anywhere I chose. The time expired without Beah's making his appearance.

On Monday, September 21st, 1868, I left Zolu, and went to Fissahbue, a town in latitude 7° 56' 09" N., and longitude 9° 50' 43" W. I was now entirely abandoned by my Mandingo guide, to grope my way to Musardu by inquiry or instinct.

Fissahbue is a double town, or a town partitioned into two parts; occupied in one by the Mandingoes, and in the other by the Boozies. It is well built and clean in appearance, with a population of three thousand inhabitants. The king, Mullebar, is a fine-looking old gentleman of fifty years, very generous-hearted; and who was the more interesting to me because he had an equal dislike to Beah.

On Saturday, September 26th, we left Fissahbue for Bokkasah. The rough features of the country moderated into extensive plains of long fields of grass, ferns, and tall palms; the hills were at a short distance, trending along in a direction west and north-west. They had also changed the character of their formation from red sandstone to granite, and I was struck to see these round and bossy masses, with their water-courses shining and trickling down their slopes. Some of their tops were thickly wooded, while small tufts or patches of grass were thinly scattered on their sides; but its brownish appearance showed that the sun had parched it in its stony bed at the first approach of the dries. West of Bokkasah, granite hills rose one above another, crowned with a dense forest. Whenever it rained, a noise resembling distant thunder was always heard. In the months of July and August, these hills are the site of a roaring cascade.

On the road, we fell in with people from all the neighboring towns, going to market. Sitting on the road-side were numbers of young women, with baskets of ground-nuts already shelled, offering them for sale.

Our pockets and every other available place were immediately filled, gratis. Such is their custom to strangers; and their gift was particularly enhanced by the repeated liberality with which both hands went down into the basket, and came up piling full, to be emptied with a gracious smile into the capacious pockets of our country coats. Then followed an exchange of compliments; and the three languages—Boozie, Mandingo, and English—got into a confusion from which smiles and brass buttons alone could deliver us.

On we went, munching ground-nuts and receiving ground-nuts, snapping fingers and making friends, and occasionally consigning Beah to evil destinies. At last the road suddenly widened, broad and clean; and the din of human voices assured us that we had come upon the market and the town.

Bokkasah is in latitude 8° 10' 02". It is a double town, similar to Fissahbue, one part of which is Boozie, and the other Mandingo. The walls that contain the Boozie portion of the inhabitants make a circuit completely oval. That which comprises the Mandingoes butts up against and flanks the eastern side of the Boozie walls, and is also half oval in shape.

On entering the town, we were shown Beah's residence. Astonished at our arrival, he forthwith tried to make some slight atonement for his former shortcomings by the diligence with which he procured us comfortable lodgings. We were soon domesticated in the town, kindling up friendships on all sides. The Mandingoes made it a point to be foremost in all these alliances. Since I was going to their country, they took me in their special charge. Among the many attentions paid me, I was invited by a young Mandingo lady to go with her to see her mother. We had no sooner arrived at the house, than she commenced calling out, "Ma, ma!" 'I waited to hear what would follow; but the next words were in musical Mandingo, informing her mother that she had brought the Tibbabue (American man) to see her. The Mandingoes use the same words in calling mother that we do. This interview ended satisfactorily in a large bowl of rice, with fried chicken, palm-wine, etc., together with a standing invitation to come to her house every day while I remained in Bokkasah.

The young lady was married to a young Mandingo by the name of Fatomah, whose father, Phillakabmah, resided at Boporu, but was then in the Barline country. The kindness and good office of this family were untiring. I also had many friends in the eastern part of the town, who were constant in their attention to me.

Bokkasah contains about fifteen hundred houses, and about seven thousand inhabitants. It is very perplexing on the first entrance of a stranger to find his way in these towns; for the houses seem to be dropped by accident into their places, rather than placed after any organized method. Chancellor, my interpreter, though well accustomed to these kind of towns, was not at all times assured of his own whereabouts. A woman gave him water to bathe; after he had performed his ablutions, he found himself naked, lost, and ashamed to ask where he was. He wandered over the town with the vessel in his hand, until some one, guessing the truth, brought him home. One does not lose his way on account of the size of these towns, but on account of the manner in which the houses are sprinkled about. You can march up to your house without knowing it, so completely does similarity and confusion repeat itself.

The market of Bokkasah, which is held every Saturday, is one of the principal markets in the Domar country. It is attended by six or seven thousand people. The articles of exchange are numerous. It is also a great country cloth market. In all these markets throughout the Boozie and Barline countries, the small country cloth known among us as the trade country cloth is not to be seen. It is owing to the mischievous industry of our friends at Boporu and its vicinity that these country cloths are reduced to so small a size. It is the business of these interlopers in trade to take large country cloths to pieces, and make them smaller. Similar is their dealing with every species of trade, to its great diminution and discouragement. If the interior trade amounted to millions of dollars in value to the republic, it could never reach our seaport towns while the border of our influence has been removed by tribal interference and war, and confined to the very seacoast settlements themselves. These obstructions can only be removed by the energetic action of government.

Bokkasah is a town very convenient and cheap for living. Abundance of vegetables, rice, beans, potatoes, plantains, bananas, ground-nuts, etc., are to be had at all times at the daily market.

While I was staying here, I dispatched one of my Congoes to Begby, a Mandingo chief, living at a town called Bokkadu, near the Boondee country, in a westward direction. As he was anxious to see some one who had come from an American town, and in American dress, I tried to gratify him in that respect. This Congo, before he reached Bokkadu, crossed the St. Paul's River on a bridge of wicker-work, and the Cape Mount River, which was much wider, on a corkwood float. This journey occupied three days. Both of these rivers flow from the north-east.

Among some of the singular institutions that prevail in this country, is a kind of convent for women, in the mysteries of which every woman has to be instructed. What these mysteries are I have never been fully informed. They consist in the main of a peculiar kind of circumcision and of certain other practices necessary for health. Attached to the outer wall of the town are the houses, fenced in on all sides from the gaze of passers-by, and especially excluded against the entrance of men. It is death to any man to be caught within the precincts, which is instantly inflicted without reprieve by the women themselves.

There are, however, holidays in which the rigid rules of the institution are relaxed, and every body is permitted to go in and see their friends without distinction of sex. During my stay here, one of these holidays occurred, and I was invited to visit the sacred grounds of this female mysticism. It consisted of rows of long huts built low to the ground, the lodgings of the devotees. Each complement belonging to a hut were seated in a line, in front of their dwellings, on a mat. Their heads were wound round with enormous turbans, and their bodies decked out in all the finery their friends in town could afford. They kept their heads hanging down in a solemn manner. Even children, six or seven years of age, were included in this moping, surly observance. Their friends from town crowded around, delighted at the sight, and with unfeigned pleasure asked me if it was not fine. I should have been more pleased to have heard these women and children laughing and singing in their rice and cotton-farms, than to have seen them tormenting themselves with a senseless, morose custom. I was carried into one of their establishments, and made to shake hands with my moody sisters.

As I have before related, this was the town in which my Mandingo guide, Beah, and all his family resided. Three days after my arrival, he disappeared, pretending he had immediate business at Salaghee, leaving word with the town-people not to allow me to go anywhere until he returned. I was determined to free myself from his tricks, and I exposed to his friends his dealings with me when I was at Zolu. His friends, and especially his mother and sisters, besought me to wait for him. After a week had expired, I grew impatient to start; but the whole family of women came, crossing their hands, and placing themselves in the most suppliant attitudes, crying, "Ejung, Ejung"—I beg you! I beg you! These poor women were honest, and knew nothing of their relation's crooked dealings. They made use of various ways to reconcile me to further delay. I had now been at Bokkasah three weeks, and had been foiled in every attempt to get away. The sort of hinderances through which I had now to struggle were not downright tyrannical opposition; they were of a more powerful and moral kind; supplications based upon kindness and generosity.

About this time an old Mandingo priest whom I had met at Bessa's town arrived. After he had been in town two days, he sent for me, and appeared glad to see me. I related to him the difficulties I experienced from Beah's actions. He advised me to be careful, and not to force my way through the country, as there had been a plot made to hurt me; and he went on to make many dark and pregnant insinuations. He exhorted me to patience and prayer, the contraries of which I had been provoked to by the artifices of Beah, and the consequent delays he had occasioned me. The next day the Mandingo priest told me that I had better make a "Sallikah," which is an offering to good luck. This offering was dictated by the priest himself. It was to be a sheep, a penknife, a white country cloth, and ten white kola. Not knowing what divinity was to be appeased, I refused to make the sacrifice or oblation; for this priest was subsisting on a dry vegetable diet, the hospitality of his stingy brethren, and he was poor, very poor. The sacrifice or offering was to be delivered to him to be buried in the ground. But who could not see the crafty old priest and his hungry students in a congratulatory chuckle over a fat sheep, a penknife, a country cloth, and a fool of a Tibbabue?

This sort of priest is numerous, needy, cunning, and mischievous; they distribute themselves in all the towns between Musardu and Boporu; and they did not fail to present themselves to me throughout the journey as "god-men." But I gave them plainly to understand that I was not to be gulled by their practices.

I now dissembled my anxiety to depart, putting on a semblance of cheerfulness to abide where I was, and a perfect indifference about going anywhere. Every afternoon I would dress myself in my Mandingo toga, and go in the eastern part of the town to visit my friends. Here we would fritter away the time in talking and singing, and I musically entertained several of my Mandingo friends with the beauties of "Dixie." We would then clap into our prayers, they repeating the Fatiha, and I reciting the Lord's Prayer. A young lady begged that I would write off this prayer for her, in order that she might have it to wear around her neck, as well as to have fillets made of it to bind around her temples, as she was sometimes troubled with the headache. I wrote it off for her; but I made her understand, at the same time, that its efficacy consisted in healing the ailments of the soul, and not of the body. While we were thus handsomely enjoying ourselves, the terrible Dowilnyah sent his messengers for me to come and see him.

Dowilnyah is the king of the Wymar Boozies. His messengers were tall black men, with red and restless eyes, tattooed faces, filed teeth, huge spears, and six feet bows. They also had a reputation which remarkably corresponded with their appearance.

A discussion arose as to the safety of my going, and it caused a disagreement that ended in the return of the messengers without me. In a week's time the messengers returned again. I had resolved to go with them. But my friends did all they could to dissuade me. Many of Dowilnyah's atrocities were repeated to me; how, when he had suspected the fidelity of one of his wives, he compelled her to pound the child of her supposed illicit connection in a mortar; how he had wantonly shot one of his wives, remarking, as he did so, that he had only shot a dog; his terrible cruelty to his prisoners whom he captured in war; and even his cruelty to his own children, one of whom he threw among the drivers, (*termites bellicosi*,) and which was so mutilated by these voracious insects that the child lost one of its arms. He had no peer in cruelty and wickedness except Comma, who was now dead, but who, when living, went hand in hand with him in evil deeds. Comma's town, it must be remembered, was the place where Seymore had his right hand nearly slashed off.

I, however, left Bokkasah for Dowilnyah's on Monday, the 2d of November, 1868, and arrived at Ukbaw-Wavolo, a village at which he was residing, on Thursday, the 5th of November, 1868.

Before reaching this village, we halted in our journey at Nubbewah's town. It was well built, clean, and strongly fortified. We were brought into the presence of Nubbewah, the chief. He was an old man; tall, or rather long—as he was lying down—thin, and looked to be much emaciated by sickness. It was difficult to arouse him from the lethargic insensibility into which he had fallen. His attendants, however, succeeded in awakening him to the fact of our presence; but, as we still seemed to be regarded as a dream, I thought proper to quicken his consciousness by blazing away with my revolver against his earthen walls. This act perfectly startled him into a proper regard for our dignity and welfare, and thereupon we were well fed, comfortably lodged, and liberally presented with mats and country cloths, etc.

On Wednesday, we traveled until we reached Boe, a very large town belonging to the Wymar Boozies. This town, with some outlying villages, is the beginning of the Wymar country, which is separated from the Domar by a narrow creek, acknowledged as a boundary. The village where the king was staying is E.N.E. of Boe, and about two and a half hours' walk from that town.

A temporary misunderstanding between the king and some of his chiefs had caused him to reside in this secluded hamlet.

It appears that Boe had been threatened with an attack from the Domar Boozies. Succor was immediately requested from Dowilnyah, who quickly marched from his capital, Gubbewallah, to the defense of Boe. He succeeded in defeating the Domars. But during his residence at Boe, so overshadowing was his influence and power, that the subordinate chiefs found themselves nearly stripped of the authority they were accustomed to exercise. A general dissatisfaction ensued, on which the king became so indignant that he withdrew from Boe, drawing in his train every thing that rendered that town attractive and important. He remained deaf to every solicitation to return. And here, at this village, he held his court, giving audience to the messengers of interior chiefs, granting favors, adjusting disputes. The village was alive with the chiefs of other towns, messengers going and coming, fine-looking women, warriors, etc.

When we drew near the village, we were requested by our guides to discharge our pieces, in order to inform the king of our arrival. This being done, we entered. The king, seated on a mat, was dressed in a gaudy-figured country robe; on his head was a large blue and red cloth cap, stuck all over with the talons of large birds. At his side was seated his chief counselor, whose name was Jebbue, a man of very large proportions, but of a mild and gentle countenance. The king was surrounded by his people, all variously dressed in white, blue, striped, and yellow country coats.

His countenance assured us that he had not been misrepresented, notwithstanding his effort to compose it in a peaceful manner. It was one of the most threatening and the blackest visages I had seen for some time. He bade me welcome. A mat was then spread, upon which we seated ourselves. Suddenly his iron horns and drums sounded, his warriors rushed forth from their concealed places, performing all the evolutions of a savage and barbarous warfare. The thundering plaudits of the people themselves increased the din. After this tremendous flourish had subsided, the king arose, and stepping forward, he waved his right hand in all directions, announcing by that gesture the uncontrolled authority with which he reigned in his dominions. Being welcomed again and again to his country, we were shown to our lodgings, which, though just temporarily erected, were comfortable.

Friday, 6th of November, 1868, I visited the

king. Stating that we had come to see his country, and to make ourselves well acquainted with him and all his people, we then delivered our presents, which consisted of a piece of calico; a music-box, with which he was especially pleased; two pocket handkerchiefs, one pair epaulets, two bottles cologne, one clasped knife, three papers needles, one large brass kettle. He was delighted; he told me that I should not regret my visit to his country; and come who would after me, I should always hold the first place in his estimation; that he had been informed of all that had been said against him to prevent my coming to see him; but as I had disregarded these reports, he would show me that my confidence had not been misplaced.

He was anxious to see my revolvers, the fearful reputation of which preceded me everywhere I went. They were shown; their use explained, and their effect exaggerated. When he had also seen the astronomical instruments, his courage entirely forsook him. He requested me to give him some medicine to prevent his enemies from poisoning him. I replied that I had no such medicine; that by exercising the proper precaution in eating and drinking, he might be able to escape the evil intention of his enemies.

He next requested me to fire my muskets, that he might see the mysteries of a cap-gun; and he caused all the broken pieces of the exploded caps to be gathered and preserved. I had to take some pains to dismiss his apprehensions that I would hurt him in any way.

He celebrated my visit to his country by a wardance. He commenced it with some of his old habits, in which, however, palm-wine flowed instead of blood. After he had supped off about a quart of that beverage, he retired to his residence, and in the lapse of fifteen minutes, the clamor of his people and his war-drums signified his reappearance. He came forth with wild and prodigious leaps; a war-cap of leopard-skin, plumed with horse-hair, covered his head; he was naked to the waist, but wore a pair of Turkish-shaped trowsers. He had a large spear in his right hand. His dress and enthusiasm had completely metamorphosed him. His black and lowering countenance had undergone a terrible change, which was heightened by the savage grin which his white teeth imparted to it. The most frantic gestures now took place, amid the stunning plaudits of the whole town.

This being ended, the king called upon his women to give the finishing stroke to this happy business.

The ladies of Wymar are fond of dancing, and they spend much of their time in this amusement: they are not acquainted with the polite and delicate paces of their sisters at Monrovia; but for downright solid-footed dancing, they can not be surpassed. They are all fine, large, robust women, and have the happiest-looking countenances in the world.

African rulers in these parts travel very leisurely from one point to another, and at every intermediate place where they may halt, are sure to spend as much time as would be necessary to carry them to their final destination. This careless, lounging habit of wasting time is an incurable one; arguments or persuasion strengthened by gifts can not overcome it.

The king had informed me of his intention to leave

this village for his own town; the very day was appointed He did not leave, however, until two days afterward. On Tuesday, 10th November, the king requested me to fire my muskets, in order to announce to the neighboring towns and villages his departure. He preferred my guns, because their report was louder than the cracking of his little English fusees, many of which I was assured had come to him by the way of Musardu through the Mandingoes.

At ten o'clock we started, the king being attended by his friends, body-guard, musicians, and women. Happily the town to which we were going lay on the road direct to Musardu. About three o'clock we came to Ziggah Porrah Zue, the largest town and the capital of the Wymar country. The king before entering the town made a halt to put on his robes. Every body dressed themselves. I was even requested to put on my uniform, which I did. After much firing and music, we entered, amid the applause and gaze of the whole town. After we had passed the gate and traversed the town some distance, we found ourselves encountered by another gate and wall; this contained the middle town. We passed on, and soon arrived at the gate and wall of the central town. Thus there are three towns, with their walls concentrically arranged. The inner walls were, however, much dilapidated, and served only to show in what manner the whole town had been successively enlarged; for as soon as an outside wall had been built around the new outside town, the inner wall was suffered to decay. The exterior or outside wall, though of great extent, was in good repair. We were conducted to the market-space in the central town, which was spacious and convenient for holding large crowds. Some arrangement and order being introduced, a speech of welcome was delivered by the old chief of the town, Dowilnyah's uncle. At the conclusion, every trumpet, consisting of forty pieces, sounded. The band of ivory and wood belonged to the town; and it must be confessed that though the execution was simple, in effect it was really fine. Many speeches were made, the end of which was always concluded with music from the bands. These three bands did not all play at the same time, but successively, one after another, the king's band being allowed the precedence.

After speech-making came the war-dances of the principal chiefs, the women cheering them on. Each chief, as soon as he had performed his part, was immediately saluted by the king's body-guard, who, marching forward to meet him, acknowledged by that act his valor and achievements. Dowilnyah closed the festivities by exhibiting his own warlike prowess. We were assigned our lodgings. Every day we passed in this town was given to festivity and enjoyment.

One of their chief amusements was a "jack upon stilts," a fellow fantastically dressed, wearing a false face, and mounted upon stilts ten feet high fitted to the soles of his feet—with which he danced, leaped, and even climbed upon the houses. He was full of clownish tricks and sayings, and made much sport for the crowds; he belonged to the king's train, a sort of king's fool. The women are really the industrious part of the population; for while their lords are wholly devoted to pleasure, palavers, and wars, the women are engaged in numerous domestic duties, and especially in spinning cotton. Here, also, as in the Domar country, the spindle is in the hands of every woman, from the princess to the slave. The women, however, enjoy themselves, particularly on market-days, which at this town takes place every Sunday.

This market is seated on the banks of the St. Paul's River, and is carried on under the shade of large cotton (bombax) and acacia-trees. The commodities of exchange are country cloths, cotton stripes, raw cotton, iron, soap, palm-oil, palm-butter, ground-nuts, rice, plantains, bananas, dried fish, dried meat, peas, beans, sweet potatoes, onions, (chalots,) snuff, tobacco, pipes, salt, earthen pots or vessels for holding water and for cooking purposes, large quantities of Kola slaves, and bullocks. The bullocks are generally brought by the Mandingoes to the market. Palm-wine is not allowed to be sold in the market. Peace and order are secured by persons especially appointed for that purpose. After every body has assembled on the ground, these preservers of the peace with long staves in their hands go through the market, ordering every body to sit down; they then admonish the people to carry on their bargains peacefully and without contention. This preliminary being gone through with, the market is opened. It is generally attended by six or seven thousand people. There are several large markets held in the Wymar country; the one at Comma's town is larger than this. The daily market held in the central town is very convenient for making small purchases.

On Saturdays, sitting under the shade of large

acacia-trees, I have watched the almost uninterrupted stream of people with their bundles and packs coming from every neighboring town and village to market. The bridge crossing the St. Paul's River would be laden or occupied from one end to the other, for hours, but it proved equal to the purpose for which it was built. When the Mandingoes would arrive with their cattle, they would swim them across, but always experience difficulty in getting them up this side of the bank, on account of its steepness. No one seemed to think of remedying this inconvenience by sloping a pathway for the animals.

The bridge is a simple structure of wicker-work. From each side of the river the ends of the bridge depend from a stout branch of an acacia-tree. The roadway is of plaited ratan, two feet wide, and worked up on both sides about four and a half feet, to prevent falling over. It is further steadied and supported by a great number of strong and flexible twigs, which connect the bottom and the sides to every available limb of the trees growing on each bank. It is ascended by ladders; its elevation is from twenty-three to twenty-five feet from the surface of the river, and spans a length of eighty-five feet.

Ziggah Porrah Zue, the capital of the Wymar country, is in latitude 8° 14' 45"; longitude, 9° 31'. Its elevation is about 1650 feet above the level of the sea. The barometer standing from 28.08 to 28.12. Thermometer ranging from 67° to 92° from November 14th to November 30th. It is seated on the St. Paul's River. The large market is held between the river and the wall of the town. I am informed that this river runs

N. E. by E. into the Mandingo country, and that it takes its rise at the foot of some hills in that country. The Little Cape Mount River takes a similar direction; but in point of size, and in the number of its tributary creeks, it is superior to the St. Paul's.

The highest point of the slope or declivity of land from Monrovia to Ziggah Porrah Zue is from 1600 to 1700 feet above the level of the sea for a distance of latitude 116 miles. It is impossible that rivers thus situated should be any thing else but the drains of a country, and their course a series of cataracts and falls.

Every afternoon the king's body-guard performed their military evolutions. They had three war-drums, one of which was bound around with three tiers of human jaw-bones. A double-quick was beaten, to which they kept time for about half an hour, without tiring. They would then enter upon more violent motions, which were more of an athletic than a military kind. They were armed with English fusees, and heavy iron cutlasses of native manufacture. Their war-dress consisted of leopard-skins.

The Bonsie country is densely populated. The difference between the Domar and Wymar Boozie is, that the latter marks his face from his temple to his chin with an indelible blue stain, while the former does not practice tattooing of any kind. This tribe extends from the south-west portion of the Pessy country to the western border of the Mandingo country.

Dowilnyah now proposed to forward me on to Musardu under his protection—and a more powerful protection could not be obtained. His own nephew

4*

was to accompany me. We left Ziggah Porrah Zue November 30th, 1868, taking a direction E.N.E. The country was open and covered with tall grass, canebrake, and wild rice. In an hour's walk we came to the town where the king formerly resided, Gubbewallah, meaning Sassa-wood tree, referring to a large old tree that grew in the middle of the town.

We passed on, and halted at Pellezarrah—meaning several paths, because several paths crossed each other near the town.

Several large cotton-trees grew at the junction of these roads. The features of the country are hilly, but the slopes are longer and more gentle. One large hill had a gradual slope of nearly two miles, while its opposite side came down in a perpendicular line. Trees now indeed began to be scarce, the country being covered with cane-brake, wild rice, and very tall palm-trees. Some trees of that short, stunted species which grow on our beach at the Cape, were seen sparsely scattered here and there. We traveled over a hard soil of red clay, pebbles, and iron ore. The tall grass and treeless slopes, plains, and hills led my Congoes to declare that I had missed the route, and walked into the Congo country; and they commenced to thank me for returning them into their country Mesumbe. We halted at Pezarrah at six o'clock P.M.; This town had suffered from fire in one part, and was being rebuilt. The whole direction traveled was E.N.E. Tuesday, 1st December, 1868, we started from Pellazarrah. After a walk of a quarter of an hour, the road led through a district which was a solid mass of iron ore. A short reddish grass struggled for existence on this extensive plain of metal.

The iron was so pure that the road leading through it was a polished metal pathway, smoothed over by the constant treading of travelers. It is said to be hardly treadable in the dries, it becomes so thoroughly heated. We occupied three and a half hours in passing over these hills and plains of metal. We afterward came to high grass, through which some elephants had just passed. The palm-trees entirely cease. We halted at Ballatah at three o'clock P.M.

Wednesday, 2d December, 1868, at Ballatah. This is one of the most pleasantly situated of all the Boozie towns we had visited. The people insisted on our spending a day with them, that they might have some time to look at us. They killed a sheep, and furnished rice and other things in abundance. They then tried to prevail on me to undertake an elephant-hunt with them. Elephants are plentiful and large in this portion of the country, and every night they could be heard making a noise, while regaling themselves on the tender cotton-plants growing in the farms of the Ballatah people.

Artemus Ward declares that "Every man has his fort." It is not mine to hunt elephants—especially to hunt elephants going in herds of ten or twelve, and that in an open country like Ballatah. I therefore declined the invitation to go on an elephan.-hunt, telling my friends that I would postpone the pleasure to be derived from such amusements until I returned from Musardu.

Ballatah is in latitude 8° 17' 51". Its approximate elevation is about two thousand feet above the level of the sea; barometer standing 27.172. It is not so large as the other Boozie towns, but far better laid out. The houses are not crammed so closely together. It contains about twenty-five hundred people; it is seated in a plain, and is commanded by very high and abrupt hills on its western side, while the land rolls off in gentle undulations toward the east. We were carried to some outlying villages north-west of Ballatah, situated at the foot of the same high hills that overlook that town. Here they were busy smelting iron. The furnaces were built of clay, and of a conical shape, from five and a half to six feet high, having clay pipes or vents close to the bottom, arranged in groups of two and three, for the purpose of draught. The charcoal and iron ore are put in at the top. At the bottom is an opening through which the slag and other impurities are withdrawn.

Thursday, December 3d, 1868, we started from Ballatah. The direction was N.E., and parallel to a range of very high hills, called the Vukkah hills. These hills are from seven hundred to one thousand feet high, and are variously composed of granite, iron ore, and a reddish clay which, from the steep slopes near the top, had shelved down in many places. The whole country, hill and plain, was covered with long grass and canebrake, interspersed with a short, dwarfish tree. The bark of this tree is rough and corrugated, the trunk is a foot in circumference, eight or ten feet high; and has an excessive branching top. The leaves small, and of an oval shape. Clumps of large trees occupied the sides and knolls of the hills.

These hills are of all sizes, and run in every direction. Toward the N. and N.E., a line of hills towers above the rest, the ridge of which makes a variety of outline against the sky. These hills are not so ruggedly disposed as those in the Domar country. The slopes are gentler; only near the summit they sometimes change feature, taper off to a point, or go right up perpendicularly. To these hills and fastnesses the natives resort in time of war, carrying all their effects, their wives and children, to the most inaccessible parts. Judging from a hill which was shown me as being used for that purpose, some of them must be very safe retreats.

Agriculture in this country must be a very simple and easy process. No "cutting farm," as we call it, by felling trees and cutting undergowth. The soil, though covered with tall grass and canebrake, is one of the highest fertility. When the sun has sufficiently parched the tall grass, it is sometimes burnt off, sometimes cut down and hoed in for manure. Farms of hundreds of acres can be prepared in a very short time; and the natives, with their small hoes, can well afford to have the large plantations of rice, cotton, and millet, which we saw.

Friday, 4th of December, 1868, we rested at Vukkah. This town stands at the foot of a range of high hills of the same name. It is the last Boozie town, and the nearest to the Mandingo country. These hills, called "Vukkah" by the Boozies, and " Fomah" by the Mandingoes, take a definite direction N.E. They are the highest range, and form a marked and acknowledged boundary between the Boozie and Mandingo territories. At the foot of this range are seated a number of towns, Boozie and Mandingo.

The town of Vukkah was overgrown with wild cane and plantain-trees. The houses were dilapidated, presenting a disagreeable contrast to the usual neatness of the Boozie towns. The inhabitants are the most ill-favored of all the Boozies. This town is also notorious for the mischief and trouble it gives thoroughfarers; and but for our coming under the protection of Dowilnyah, it soon fell out what would have happened. We had not been in the town an hour before we had a row with one of the principal men of the place. He requested me to fire my musket, which I did a number of times, sufficient, as I thought, to please every body; but he insisted on several more rounds. I refused; he then told me to go on to Musardu, but when I returned I would find that my way home would not lie through that town. I was, however, under too powerful a protection to be disturbed. Dowilnyah was not to be trifled with. To take a head from a shoulder was mere pastime with him.

Much allowance, however, must be made for these African rulers. Tyrannical and bloodthirsty they sometimes appear; but this character is artificial, and practiced in many instances to inspire terror and respect, without which they could not hold their authority a single hour.

Beset by rivalships and conspiracies, they are forced, from the boisterous circumstances of their situation, to employ every means conservative of their authority and their lives.

Saturday, 5th of December, we started from Vukkah. We had now crossed the Vukkah hills, and were fairly in the Mandingo country. Many of the plains of this section of the country are terraced, one above another. Amends is made for a simple vegetation, by the ever-varying forms of relief the country presents, the farther you advance into it.

At three o'clock P.M., we were met on the road by several Mandingoes, who accompanied us to their town, Nu-Somadu, or Mahommadu. The walls of this town are quadrilateral in shape, each side being a series of bastions, which at a distance looks like some old fortified front. The walls, however, are so thin that a four-pounder could demolish them in a very little time.

We entered the town, and were entertained in a very hospitable manner. A house was given to us, small indeed in its dimensions to what we had been accustomed to in the Boozie country, but convenient and comfortable. Being wearied with the journey, I threw myself into a hammock, and commenced surveying alterations and arrangements which a change in the character of the country had introduced. The house was a circular structure of clay, with a conical roof made entirely of large canebrake and long grass. In looking around the walls, our eyes rested on a saddle, stirrups, bridle, with leather leggings, and a tremendous tower gun.

Sunday, the 6th of December, we attempted to pursue our journey; but the chief refused to allow us to depart before he had demonstrated his good-will and hospitality. He killed a heifer, and cooked it with onions. We satisfied our appetites, and made him an appropriate present. We then departed; arrived at Naalah late in the afternoon. In the morning, a trooper was at once dispatched to Musardu, to inform them that the Tibbabue (American) had come. In two hours he returned, telling me that the Musardu people requested that I would remain at Naalah until they had made preparations for my reception. I immediately sent them word that I had been so long coming to see their country that I would rather forego any public demonstration than be delayed any further. I was then answered to come on ; they would gladly receive me.

Accompanied by several Mandingoes from Naalah and Mahommadu, we started for Musardu. Our interest in the journey was enlivened by the novel features of the country. In passing through the Boozie country, extensive views were frequently obstructed by a dense vegetation that hemmed in the sight on each side of a narrow foot-path. Here the peculiar features of the country are visible for miles. The towns and villages seated in the plains, people on foot and people on horseback can be seen at a great distance, and have more the air of light, life, and activity, than many parts of the Boozie country, where the sombre gloom of immense forests conceals all such things. The large town of Du Quirlelah lay on our right, in the bosom of some small hills. It lay on our right; but from our elevated position, it might well be said to lie under us. Going on, we descried a long, whitish border, raised a little above the height of a gentle slope. On drawing nearer, it proved to be the top of the south-western wall of Musardu. We fired our muskets, and entered the town. We were led up a street, or narrow lane, that brought us into the square in which the mosque was situated. Here were gathered the king, Vomfeedolla, and the principal men of the town, to receive us. My Mandingo friends from Mahommadu opened the civilities of introduction with an elaborate speech; stating where I had come from, and for what I had come; the power, learning, and wealth of the Tibbabues. One of my friends, Barki, from Mahommadu, then engaged to swear for me, that I had come for no ill purpose whatever, but that I was moved entirely by an intelligent curiosity and friendly intercourse. Dowilnyah's messengers then spoke in flattering terms of my demeanor and liberality in their country, and the wishes of the king, in consequence, that I should be treated in every way befitting an illustrious stranger and his particular guest. I had never before been so complimented, and I became uneasy at the high importance attached to the Tibbabue visit, fearing that great expectations in the way of dashes or presents might be disappointed. For my bundles, bulky and pretentious in appearance, contained books, instruments, and clothes, more than the means upon which many hopes were then founding and growing. After the speeches were over, the king and his people gave me repeated welcomes, with the peculiar privilege of doing at Musardu whatever I was accustomed to do at Monrovia, a large liberty, granted only to distinguished strangers. An infinite number of salaams and snapping of fingers then followed. I was soon disposed of, with luggage and carriers, in the king's court-yard, with a house similar in structure and accommodation to the one at Mahommadu. We had learned the art of domiciling ourselves in these towns, and in fifteen minutes every thing wore the appearance of our having lived there for years. A number of Mandingo girls came to sing and dance for us, and we wasted some powder by way of returning the compliment.

As soon as night came on, we retired to rest; but our slumbers were disturbed by a harper, who, in a tremulous minor key, improvised that since Musardu had been founded such a stranger had never visited it. The harp itself was a huge gourd, and a most unmusical "shell" it proved to be. It had three strings, the thrummings of which disquieted me on two accounts. First, the noise, intrinsically disagreeable. Secondly, the expectations which that noise might be raising, as the bard in his *nocturne* declared my many gracious qualities, my courage, my wealth, and my liberality; upon the last two he dwelt with loud and repeated effort.

King Vomfeedolla in appearance has a mild, gentle countenance. His features would please those who are fond of a straight nose, broad forehead, thin lips, large and intelligent eyes, and an oval chin. Like all the Mandingoes, his skin is a smooth, glossy black. In stature he is rather below the general towering height of this tribe. He does not possess the fiery energy of his royal Boozie brother, Dowilnyah, who, though many years his senior, far excels him in that respect.

In all councils Vomfeedolla seems to be entirely a listener, and to be directed and influenced by the older members of the royal family. He is said to be a great warrior; but the evidences around Musardu prove that if he is, he must belong to the unfortunate class of that profession.

The usual apparel or dress of the Mandingoes consists of four pieces—two pieces as a shirt and vest, an one large coat or toga worn over all; one pair of Turkish-shaped trowsers coming a little below the knees: sandals for the feet, which are sometimes beautifully worked; and a three-cornered cap for the head. These articles, made and worn as a Mandingo *only* can make and wear them, leave nothing to be desired, either as to taste and utility. This is said so far as the men are concerned. But I must deplore a fashion observed by the women, in wrapping up their faces and bodies in a manner truly ungraceful, and unhealthy, too.

Musardu is an exceedingly healthy place; there was not one prostrate, sickly person in the town. There is, however, a disease which sometimes attacks individuals in a peculiar way; it is an affection of the throat, causing a protuberance almost similar to what is called the "king's evil." I inquired the cause, and they imputed it to something that impregnates the water during the height of the dry season, being the time when it mostly seizes persons.

The atmosphere of Musardu is very dry, and had a very favorable effect upon my watches, which were declared at Monrovia to be out of order; but as soon as I reached Musardu, every one of them began to tick away in a clear and ringing manner.

Musardu, the capital of the Western Mandingoes, is in latitude 8° 27′ 11″ N., longitude 8° 24′ 30″ W.; it is elevated two thousand feet above the level of the sea, and is situated amid gentle hills and slopes. North and north-east two very high hills tower above the rest several hundred feet. The population is between seven and eight thousand, but the many villages and hamlets increase it to a greater proportion. In the days of its prosperity, and before it had suffered from the damaging effects of war, it had occupied a larger space, and was not surrounded by any wall. Though it has lost its former importance, Musardu is still considered as the capital of the Western Mandingoes, and its name is never mentioned but in terms of patriotism and respect. I often heard the old men of the town regret its past power and wealth. They told me that what I then saw of Musardu was only the ruins of a former prosperity. The town is laid off irregularly, with very narrow and sometimes winding lanes or streets. These lanes or streets cross each other in such a way as to give access to any part of the town. The houses are built facing the lanes, and the rear space is used as a yard for horses and cattle. In the south-western part of the town is the mosque. The walls having been injured by the weather, they had commenced to repair it. It is a quadrilateral building, surrounded by an oval-shaped wall, which is carried up eight feet, and upon which rest the rafters of a large [conical thatch-roof. The interior space is thirty-two feet long and twenty-two feet wide, and nine feet high. It is laid off in four compartments, by three intermediate walls running the length of the building. These separate spaces communicate with each other by three doors or openings in each intermediate wall. I do not know the purpose of the divisions, unless it is to grade the faithful. It can scarcely accommodate more than one hundred and twenty persons, and must therefore be devoted to the most pious, or the leaders or teachers of Islam.

On Monday, the 14th of December, 1868, the King

Vomfeedolla held a military demonstration. He had summoned his infantry and cavalry from the nearest towns of Billelah, Yokkadu, Naalah, and Mahommadu. The exercises commenced about two o'clock P.M., in the large square of the town. The spectators and musicians had already assembled. All at once a trooper dashed past at full speed, as if he was reconnoitring the enemy. Several others followed, dispersing in different directions. The position of the enemy seeming to be determined, they soon returned. The trumpet then sounded, and a grand cavalry charge took place. Riding up in line, with musket in hand, they would deliver their fire, and canter off to the right and left, in order to allow the rear lines to do the same. As soon as the firing was over, they slung their muskets, and, rising in the saddle, drew their long knives in one hand and their crooked swords in the other; the horse, now urged to a headlong gallop by the voice, carries his rider, standing in the stirrups, with furious velocity into the heat of the battle. Such are the evolutions of the Mandingo cavalry. Their equipment is quite complete. They use saddles and bridles, and a peculiar and powerful bit; short stirrups; leather leggings, to which iron spurs are attached. The cavalry from all the towns, according to various reports, ought to amount to fifteen hundred.

In their open country, where the action of cavalry is greatly facilitated by the long, gentle slopes, and wide, treeless plains, they would be no mean enemy. They often dismount, in order to act on foot. Each horse has a boy attendant to take care of him while his master is thus engaged. In real action, I have been informed, the little boys of the defeated party often suffer the penalty of their participation. Yet these dangers do not deter the little fellows from going; for they are frequently able to ride off the field as soon as any symptoms of defeat are perceived.

The king seems to act for the most part with the infantry, for he rode in front and led them on. They came in deep array, and with great clamor, but without organization, being directed solely by a flag or ensign of blue cloth. I was sorry that I had no flag of ours to present them.

After their exercises were over, they requested us to fire our muskets; upon which we delivered regular volleys with bayonets fixed, both to their astonishment and delight, caused by the quickness with which we loaded our pieces, our certainty of fire—unlike their fusees, which were continually snapping—and the deeper report of our guns. As soon as all the exercises were finished, the king then distributed the presents I had given him to the chiefs of the several military divisions.

Tuesday, the 15th of December, 1868. My Mandingo friends began to press me to trade with them. I informed them that I had nothing to trade with; that my gifts to the king and the principal men of the town had exhausted my means so closely as to scarcely leave me sufficient to enable me to return home. Nothing could convince them that I had not pieces of handkerchiefs and calicoes concealed in my bundles. They tried every method to induce me to trade; they carried me to their houses and would get out their small leathern bags; these bags contained from ten to fifteen large twisted gold rings, ("sannue.") They then offered me horses, and finally concluded by offering to sell me some pretty female slaves. I informed them that the Tibbabues did not keep slaves; that I had not come to trade, but merely to visit their country; that upon my return home I would persuade my people to come and trade with them. At the prospect of a number of Tibbabues coming to their country to trade, they were exceedingly satisfied.

From trade we passed to war and politics, and having satisfied all their inquiries in these two particular points with respect to the Tibbabues, they made me acquainted with some of their wars and feuds. They had a special cause of grievance against a certain Mandingo chief whose name was Ibrahima, or Blamer Sissa, and who lived north-east, and three days' walk from Musardu, at a large town called Madina.

It appears that Blamer Sissa came from Madina to visit his uncle, Amalah, who was then residing at Musardu, and that he was treated with great civility and distinction by the Musardu people; that being a powerful young prince, they solicited his aid against some Kaffres, or unbelievers, living over the eastern hills; that in compliance with their solicitation he went back to Madina, and soon returned to Musardu, bringing with him his cavalry and infantry, a numerous and formidable mass, who, in the end, came nigh doing their friends at Musardu as much evil as they had done the Kaffres, whom they had mutually agreed to plunder.

Blamer Sissa stripped Musardu of every thing valuable, and even carried off nearly all the pretty young women of that town.

On Thursday, the 16th of December, 1868, at seven o'clock P.M., Chancellor came running to my house to inform me that several suspicious persons, with their horses or jackasses, were lurking about the north-western side of the town; that they had sought admittance, but it had been refused them; that they had reported themselves traders, but the town people were on the alert, believing them to be Blamer Sissa's spies, who were only skulking around in order to gain all the intelligence they could, and carry it to their friends, who were supposed to be in strong force behind the north-eastern hills. Next morning, Friday, the 17th of December, the strange people were indeed seen on a hill north-west of the town, and cold must have been the sleep they had of it the previous night, for the thermometer stood at 52° at four A.M. A council was held to decide how to act. Some proposed to send the young men out to kill them. Afterward it was more wisely determined to go out and order them to take their traffic and depart with it at once.

We accordingly went out, and after the usual salutations, they were given plainly to understand that neither they nor their trade could enter Musardu, and that they must depart without delay. But our strange merchants were not to be frightened off in that manner. They insisted that they had come for no evil purpose whatever, but simply to prosecute their trade. The conferences were prolonged until midday. While the conversation was going on, I had an opportunity to survey the suspicious group of new-comers. It consisted of two sturdy little jackasses, with enormous packs, containing what looked like, and afterward proved to be French blue baft, and five men. The one who acted as guide and interpreter was one of Blamer Sissa's people, and he alone served to confirm our suspicions. The other four were tall, black, good-featured people. One of them had his face and head bound up with a piece of white cotton, after the peculiar manner of some of the Arabs of the desert. They were all Mohammedans. I learned that they had come from the Senegal, had been to Futtah, passed through Kanghkah, and had obtained this guide from Madina, to show them to Musardu. I began to be interested in them. The Musardu people, however, remained deaf to every argument, and the Senegal merchants were compelled to pack their bundles on their asses, and go. Nay, the town people, to assure themselves of their going, followed them some distance. But the sight of such large bundles in such a time of need and self-interest, had sown the seeds of discord; and there was much contention now among the Musardu people themselves. Some were for allowing the merchants to enter the town. Others opposed it, alleging that such were always the artifices of Blamer Sissa when he wished to take a strong town; that he always sent some of his people ahead, who, under pretext of wishing to trade, introduced themselves into the town in order to open the gates at night to his forces. The contention grew so warm that they even came to blows.

On Saturday, the 19th of December, about nine o'clock A.M., news came to the town that the merchants had returned. We went out and found it really so; and when the order was repeated to them to go away, they absolutely refused, declaring that they had come to trade; that having left neither mother nor wife behind, the Musardu people might kill them if they wished to do so. Their firmness overcame the first determination of the Musardu people, who, after nearly having another quarrel among themselves, gave the merchants leave to trade outside of the town—a permission with which our Senegal friends seemed to be quite satisfied. It was difficult at the first to make out who our merchants were No one could understand their language except the Mandingo interpreter from Madina, and it was this man who caused them to be seriously suspected, for he was one of Blamer Sissa's soldiers. These poor merchants, therefore, might have been subserving Blamer Sissa's purposes, without the least knowledge of it themselves. It was solely their interpreter that marked them as suspected persons.

On Monday, the 21st of December, our Musardu friends, after all their blustering determination against the merchants, admitted them into the town. Interest and avarice overcame all their patriotism and caution. The two jackass-loads of goods, not unlike the Trojan horse, were dragged into the town, and if Blamer Sissa had any designs on Musardu, they were accomplished.

Both in policy and energy Blamer Sissa seemed superior to the Musardu people; for in addition to the trouble he had already given them, and even the recent threats he had made, he knew how to introduce his own people in the town, who could give any intelligence with respect to Musardu he might desire.

He is not the first prince who has taken a city by means of a jackass-load of merchandise. The Musardu people sent a thundering message of defiance and insult to Blamer Sissa, making the largest use of me to back it up. They sent him word that they were not at all dependent on him for trade or any thing else; that the Tibbabues were about to open trade with them, and would be their friends in peace and war; that even then a Tibbabue was negotiating that particular business in Musardu. They then took pains to exhibit the arms and means with which the destruction of Madina might sooner or later be accomplished. My muskets with their bayonets, my revolvers, and my person, were severally shown as designed for that especial object.

I was purposely questioned aloud as to the military resources of the Tibbabues: the little guns that fired any number of times without loading, and the big guns that burnt up cities at the distance of miles. I gave such answers as I hope will make Blamer Sissa less troublesome to Musardu for the future.

It might be thought impolitic that I did not refrain from expressing myself as being in either party's favor. In this part of Africa, if hostilities are lukewarm, neutrality is possible; but where it burns with the flame of recent and bitter injuries, you are absorbed by either one side or the other, or torn in pieces by both.

The Musardu people are unfortunately situated. On the north they expect war with Blamer Sissa, and on the east hostilities have never ceased; the west and south-west are still open to them. It is the latter direction that opens itself to our enterprise, and promises much to our commercial prosperity. The chief articles of trade are gold, bullocks, hides, horses, and country cloths of every variety of dye and texture. Gold is worn extravagantly by the Mandingo ladies of Musardu. Their earrings are so large and weighty as to require a narrow piece of leather to brace them up to their head-bands, so that the part of the ring in the ear may not make an unseemly hole, as sometimes happens when this necessary support is neglected. Gold is certainly abundant, and would form a lucrative trade between Musardu and Liberia. I gave twelve sheets of writing-paper (kahtahsee) and four yards of calico for a large gold twist ring. Had I came purposely to trade, and had gone through the usual practice of "jewing down," I could have purchased it for less. These rings are perfectly pure, the natives never mixing any kind of alloy in the manufacturing of them. Many of my friends wondered at my making presents of watches, music-boxes, and calicoes when the articles might have been exchanged for gold or slaves; but as I was determined that the money should be religiously appropriated to the purpose for which it was sent out, I steadily refused every proffer, excepting such few things as I could conveniently bring back as samples of the production and industry of the country.

To carry on trade safely, free from the risks and interruptions incident to a country peopled by barbarians and semi-barbarians, and divided into so many jarring interests, it would be necessary to establish four trading forts—two in the Boozie and Barline countries, which would purchase country cloths, raw cotton, camwood, rice, palm-oil, etc.; and two in the Mandingo country, where gold, bullocks, country cloths, and horses could be purchased at such rates as would amply remunerate for all the trouble, expense, and consumption of time necessary in such traffic. The individuals living in the forts would be abundantly supplied with food, as rice is produced in surplus quantities in the Boozie and Barline countries. Even the expense of clothing would be trifling, if they would use the cloth of the country. The natives declare that they would be glad to have such establishments among them. These forts would also second and strengthen any missionary effort that might be made out there; indeed, the two establishments could be made to work admirably together. The support, protection, and moral and material influence which would be exerted in the respective operations of each, would insure permanence and success. We would do well to commence the use of jackasses; indeed, it would be indispensable for the portage or transportation of luggage. The Senegal traders at Musardu carried very large packs of blue cotton on their two sturdy little animals. Horses and bullocks would form no unimportant part of the trade. Mahommadu is a regular beef-market.

The auriferous or gold district of this part of Manding is said to be principally at Buley. Upon my first inquiry, I was told that Buley was a week's journey eastward; but upon my continuing to prosecute my inquiries respecting that country, Buley was immediately removed one week's walk further, making it two weeks' walk, and through hostile and dangerous districts, the people of which, as my Musardu friends informed me, would exact toll from me for passing through their country. Every difficulty was conjured up that was conceived to be sufficient to extinguish all interest for further inquiry, or to intimidate my going in that direction.

However, my Mandingo cousins have no doubt misrepresented the whole matter; for gold not only exists at Buley, but right there in their own country—otherwise I do not think it could be so plentiful among themselves, since they have little or no communication with the east.

At Buley, it is found mixed in fine grains with the superficial deposit. No one is allowed to sweep or pick up any thing in another's yard. The gold is separated by fanning and washing; it is then smelted and twisted, and ready for sale or use. They show some skill and taste in the preparation of these rings, and they are really worth their weight in gold. Our friends are sometimes equally skillful in preparing counterfeits, as my nitric acid had several occasions to prove. Impositions of this kind are generally punished by heavy fines.

In going to Buley, you pass successively Bendalah—where a very fine species of country cloth is made, of striped figure, and usually worn by the women—Tangalah, Tutah, and Gehway. Now, if these towns are situated from each other at the usual distance of Africans—namely, a day's walk—Buley is but four days' walk east from Musardu, which I take to be the fact, despite the industry of my friends to prove to the contrary. Unlike Musardu, it is a wooded country. This fact may give us some idea of the extent of those treeless hills and plains eastward. They are said to extend further north than in any other direction, where, indeed, cow-dung is used for fuel. The population of Buley is Mandingo. Gold is also obtained north of Blamer Sissa's town, at Wasalah.

My friends now tried again to provoke me to trade, offering the same articles they had offered before—gold, horses, and female slaves. Indeed, this is all the Mandingoes of Musardu had to offer by way of trade. Not a bullock or a country cloth was to be seen, though these things are notoriously the articles of merchandise belonging to Musardu. Every thing liable to be seized in war, from its being too bulky to be quickly removed or concealed, sad experience has taught them to keep out of reach, in some friendly Boozie town in the rear of the Vukkah hills; while nothing but the war-horse, and articles easy to be hid or carried off, are kept at Musardu. At every house can be seen muskets, cutlasses, powder-horns, war-belts, and war-coats, a powerful large bow, and four or five large quivers filled with poisoned arrows. I have seen them prepare the poison with which the points of the arrows are smeared over. It is a vegetable poison, consisting of one bulbous root twice as large as an onion, and two different kinds of small vines. It is boiled in a pot to a thick or gummy consistence, the color of which is black. It is said to be so fatal that if it wounds so much as the tip end of the fingers, it is certain death. The preparers of this fearful means of savage warfare but too clearly explained to me its effects before death completely ensues: the bleeding at the nose and ears; its nauseous attack on the stomach, and consequent spitting; the final despair of the individual in lying down, with his eyes set in a vacant death-stare—all of which was imitated with a terrible fidelity to the truth, and as one of the most horrible means of barbarous warfare.

This part of Mandingo is the country of the horse. There are two sizes: the large horse, used for show and parade, and the small horse, used for war. The latter is a hardy, strong little animal, capable, in his country, of bearing great fatigue. In battle, I am informed, he kicks and bites in a furious manner, and that when his master makes a capture of a fine young lady, he willingly receives the additional burden, and gallops off faster than ever. These horses are certainly well treated and cared for; and if Musardu is not characteristic for cleanliness, it is because the horse and his master equally occupy and almost equally litter up that capital.

I tried my best to obtain some data by which an approximate notion might be formed of the age of the city; but in matters of chronology our friends have been sadly careless. None of them could give the least intelligent hint. They said that the grandfather of the oldest man in the town declared that the town was there when he was born, and that all the other towns sprang from this one. Its antiquity is an undoubted matter among themselves. I was shown their large market-place outside of the town, a few hundred yards from the south-western gate. From the space it occupied, it would easily have contained eight or ten thousand people. The respective places where each commodity was exhibited for sale was pointed out: country cloths, cattle, gold, (dust and manufactured,) slaves, grain, salt, of which there were two kinds—the slab or rock-salt, which came on camels from the north-east, and our fine salt, gotten from the coast; ostrich feathers; leather, in the beautiful and soft tanning of which the Mandingoes are particularly expert; ivory, cotton, tobacco, and an infinite variety of domestic articles were all named, and the different places where they were sold designated.

But war has abolished every sign of this commercial activity and life, and has introduced in its stead a barren space filled with weeds, grass, and the broken skulls and skeletons of enemies—a desperate battle having been fought there between the Musardu people, aided by Blamer Sissa, and the eastern Mandingoes.

The soil of the hills of Musardu is composed of reddish clay and sand, with boulders of iron ore intermixed. On the north-eastern side of the town are some large masses of black and gray granite. The plains are a whitish clay, and the very soil for a plow, being free from almost every obstruction. The light tillage of the natives never goes more than four or five inches, with their little short-handled hoes.

About February or March, and sometimes sooner, the high grass and wild cane are cut down, to rot and manure the soil. Near the planting season, these vegetable fertilizers are turned in with the hoe; and from the crops of rice, of which there are three kinds, potatoes, ground-nuts, onions, peas and beans, large gourds, corn, pumpkins, etc., it must answer abundantly the purposes of agriculture. Tobacco is grown in plots, wherever a stream of water offers itself for frequent irrigation. The rubbish and ashes of the town form excellent beds for this plant. They are generally laid out with great care, and watered three times a day.

5*

The Mandingoes are the great tobacco-raisers and snuff-makers of the country. They supply both themselves and the Boozies. Musardu is singularly free from grasshoppers, rats, and mice, owing to the number of hawks that crowd the limbs of a solitary tree that may be standing here and there. Want of trees compels them to perch themselves on rocks, and when these are all occupied, they may be seen to cover the ground in dark patches. There are also large birds that particularly belong to the grassy plains of Musardu. They go in flocks of eight or twelve. In size, they are as large as American geese, and, on account of their weight, do not fly very high, nor do they make long passages at a time. When they alight on the ground, they are enabled, by the length of their necks, to discover you before you can get within gunshot of them. Their hearing, however, is not very acute; for we have often crept up the brow of the hill, and come upon them suddenly. They are a very sagacious and shy bird; and though I and my Congoes tried our marksmanship many times, we were entirely unable to procure one of them. The Mandingoes are scarcely ever able to kill them. Their color is white, with a black band across their back and wings; and when flying, their leader never ceases to make a cawing noise. They are very gawky in their movements when walking on the ground, caused by their long necks, giving their heads a deliberative nod with every step they take.

The Mandingoes are very attentive to their farming interests. They are, however, more given to trade than to manual labor. The leading vice of a Mandingo is avarice, which, by however much it is stimulated, the present state of the country affords him but little means to gratify. Nothing can be accumulated among themselves that war does not instantly dissipate. Nevertheless, they are quick and intelligent, easy to be managed by persuasion, and they offer to Liberia a more speedy prospect of assimilation and union than any other tribe with which I am acquainted. A strong moral advantage is already gained, from their being a reading and writing people, practicing a communication of ideas and an interchange of thought by means of the Arabic. They have a natural reverence for learning and mental superiority, and they never fail to respect it, whether it accords with their belief or not. No rudeness, no indecent and wrangling intolerance, was ever shown me during my stay among them. No difference of religion ever made them diminish the respect, attention, and hospitality which they conceived were due me. One of my Congo carriers is of the Baptist persuasion, and he used to make himself heard every morning, even to my own annoyance, by loud orisons. Still, our Mohammedan Mandingoes said nothing. It was respected as a prayer, and it was known to be a Christian prayer.

On the 19th of December, I visited Billelah Kaifal, Kandah's native town. In size it is nearly as large as Musardu. The houses are in a better condition; but in all other respects it resembles the parent city—the narrow lanes, horse stables, gardens, etc. The town seemed densely populated, at least with children.

The next day we started from Billelah for our home, Musardu, visiting on our way another town, Yockkadu.

This town is about a quarter of the size of Musardu, and similar in its arrangements, customs, and habits. The chief of this town, Vawfulla, proved to be very hospitable.

On Sunday, the 21st of December, my Boozie attendants grew impatient to return home, and even prepared to leave me. I gave them full liberty to go if they wished, since I did not intend to make the least move until I had finished my business. The sky had been so hazy as to prevent my taking any observations. The fine dust of the Harmattans, together with the vast volumes of smoke and cinders from the grassy hills and plains that were burning, rendered it a difficult matter to take observations. This was the cause of my delaying to return, and the consequent dissatisfaction of my Boozies, a people who are not willing to be kept from their homes any length of time. Chancellor, however, was enabled to appease their impatience by three yards of calico.

Having now exhausted the time, as well as almost all the means which had been assigned to carry out this expedition, I began to think of returning home; yet I must confess there was nothing more contrary to my wishes. Had it not been that family responsibilities demanded my return home, I should have still, with or without means, prosecuted my journey eastward—a direction which I have always had the presentiment contains the prosperity and welfare of Liberia.

On Friday, the 25th of December, at eight A.M., we bade farewell to Musardu, and arrived at Mahommadu at six P.M. Here we passed several days, in order to take observations and to see the market. This market is held every Wednesday, outside of the eastern wall.

On Wednesday, the 30th, this market took place. It contained three hundred head of cattle, which were offered at three or four dollars a head in our money. The usual articles of rice, onions, palm-oil, cotton, country cloths, tobacco, and iron were present. There were a number of slaves for sale, especially children. A pretty little Mandingo girl, about nine years of age, was sent to my house with one of my boys, in order that I might purchase her. She cost 9000 kolu, or about $15 in our money. I was curious to know how she became a slave, as Mandingoes are seldom ever enslaved. I declined to buy her, on the ground that Tibbabues never held slaves. The child herself seemed to be disappointed; for she showed that she preferred falling into my hands in preference to her own people. The Mandingoes are harsher with their slaves than the Boozies. Among the Boozies it is difficult to distinguish the slaves by any mark of dress or usage; but the Mandingoes, though not excessively cruel, have drawn the lines of difference in so strong a manner that you can not fail to perceive them.

A great many cattle remained unsold. The season of the dries is very severe on them, and they sometimes die from overdriving. Several died the next day after the market was over. They are the large, reddish, long-horned cattle, which we usually buy from the interior. The highlands, from which they come, explains why they do not thrive so well as the black, short-horned, and sturdy cattle of the coast, known among us as the "leeward cattle."

It was at this town that I first experienced the hospitality of these people in their own country. Our Mandingoes are Mohammedans; but they have an invincible partiality for Tibbabues, who are known to be Christians, and the people of the book. It is also well known that there is some difference in the creeds or beliefs; yet the unbelieving Tibbabue is sure to be housed, fed, and befriended in a manner that is not always practiced among the faithful themselves.

While they were repairing the wall of Mahommadu, I was requested to carry some of the mortar and place it in the wall, that it might be said that "a Tibbabue helped to build these walls." I contributed all I could to make them impregnable.

During our stay there, we were also taken to their foundry, where they were busily engaged in preparing iron for the market. The pieces of pure iron taken from the furnaces are again heated; they are then reduced to a long triangular shape by pounding them with large, heavy stones—a process simple and laborious enough, and a work which is entirely left for the slaves.

Blacksmithing, such as the making of stirrups, bits, spurs, etc., is done by the Mandingoes themselves, as being a mechanical art too noble to be performed by slaves.

On Thursday, the 31st of December, we left Mahommadu, and reached Vukkah at half-past four o'clock P.M. We were now among the Boozies again. The Vukkah hills run N. E. and S.W. The towns of Mahommadu and Vukkah stand at the very foot of the south-eastern slope. I am informed that many other Mandingo and Boozie towns are situated on the same side of this range. At Mahommadu, the plain, in a south-east direction, is only interrupted by swells and rolling hills, rising and running in every direction, and marked by no particular feature, except the reddish color of the soil, and their summits ridged with the dwarfish prairie tree before mentioned. The plains are white clay, mixed with beds of iron ore. At Mahommadu, the south-east slope strikes the plain at a great angle; but at Vukkah, it rests upon a series of small table-lands that extend out a half-mile before they finally come down into the plains. The vast spaces of grass and reddish soil are relieved by patches of dense vegetation, marking the gullies and ravines. Heavy blocks of granite are set in the sides of the Vukkah hills, awaiting only to be loosened by the rains to roll from their places to the bottom. At night, the whole country seems on fire, from the burning of the grass.

On January 1st, 1869, we left Vukkah, and reached Ballatah at two P.M. On the road, we passed several streams of water, flowing over granite beds, with a temperature of 58° to 60°, Fahrenheit. We had also passed over three plains, rising one above another, in which lines of trees traced off curious plots and divisions, as if they were purposely laid out for farming. The spaces were filled in with green grass and scattering clumps of trees.

January 2d. From Ballatah, we traveled to the village of Gazzahbue.

January 3d, 1869. From Gazzahbue, we reached Gubbewallah, Dowilnyah's residence. The king was still at Ziggah Porrah Zue; but in three days he returned to his own town. Here, though anxious to hasten home, I was obliged to spend some time; since it is contrary to politeness to hurry away from the town of a great chief without having resided with him two or three weeks. All my friends who had arrived from Ziggah Porrah Zue were delighted to see me, and they began to grow solicitous about my returning to their country again. Promises of all kinds were made if I would return; promises of a very peculiar kind were made by the king if I would only return.

The ladies of Wymar seemed no less anxious respecting me; and they frequently asked me why, since I possessed the means of making so many presents, I did not have a number of women to sing and clap hands and proclaim my importance, after the fashion of their great men. To which I replied that such was not the custom of "Weegees," or Americans. They were, however, unwilling that I should go through their country "unhonored and unsung;" they therefore proposed to compliment me with this custom, and merrily fell to clapping and singing; then raising their right hands to the sky, rent the air with their acclamations of praise and flattery.

On Monday, the 25th of January, we took leave of King Dowilnyah. The king presented us with several large country cloths, and a very large and heavy ivory. He had also sent for a horse; but we declined receiving the presents, as we had no one to carry them. He would have furnished us carriers, had it not been that they would have to pass through the Domars, with whom they were not on friendly terms.

About four o'clock P.M., we reached Boe. Here we spent a day to rest. On Wednesday, the 27th January, at four o'clock P.M., we came to Nubbewah's town. King Nubbewah was not at home when we arrived; but late in the afternoon this sick and feeble old man came stalking into the town, followed by his head warrior, and a number of young men, all armed.

In the evening they held a council, and Nubbewah himself delivered a speech with a violence of gesture and voice that little corresponded with the languid, sickly frame from which it came. Mischief was brewing; but where or on whom it would first light, no one of our party could conjecture. We only hoped that it would keep to its first purposes, and not fall on us.

It was a very clear moonlight. About twelve o'clock, Chancellor, who was generally very vigilant whenever there happened to be an unusual stir among the natives, detected one of the young men, with his cutlass gleaming in the moonlight, stealthily lifting up our door-mat. He was suddenly questioned as to what he wanted, which threw him into such confusion that he was only able to stammer out something about fire, and quickly withdrew. Several persons were then seen passing and repassing in the king's court-yard. We immediately concluded that such movements boded no good to us. We aroused our party, and prepared for a general onslaught, which we every moment expected; such being the usual method of these people's attacks. Nubbewah's town contains three thousand people, men, women, and children. The houses are crowded together. The king's own department is shut off from the rest of the town by high fences, and strongly guarded with a number of large Mandingo dogs. It is every way so situated that a petty wickedness can be committed covertly and conveniently enough, and nobody be the wiser.

All the houses are bamboo, and would burn like tinder. I therefore instructed my people that, should Nubbewah attack us, we must immediately set fire to the house we were in, and discharge our muskets into those who came at us first; that amid the hubbub of fire, smoke, and fighting, our chances for escape would be as good as any one else's; that we must make for the gate nearest to our house, and march all night for Bokkasah. Our knapsacks were strapped on, our muskets in hand, and the torches blazing in the fire. There was more passing and repassing and distinct whisperings. Success with these people depends upon surprise; our bustling preparation placed a surprise entirely out of the question. In fifteen minutes all was quiet. Every one instinctively felt that the dangerous moment had passed; yet we kept on our guard.

The next morning we went to the king, who put on a most intelligent innocence. We made him a small present and immediately left his town. We arrived at Bokkasah at four o'clock P.M.

So far as the matter of carrying arms is concerned, it is always better to observe the usage of the natives. Arms always form a part of the dress of barbarians. The more formidable you can make yourself appear, the better for your peace and safety on these highways of African travel. To seem harmless does not always invoke forbearance; it sometimes suggests plots and attempts on life and property. It was that too much reliance on the simple-heartedness and good feelings of untutored barbarians that got Seymore's right hand nearly slashed off. It is preferable to try every way to induce their good-will, and at the same time to appear to be ready to resist their ill-will. Every person I met on the road was girded with a heavy iron sword, a quiver thrown over the shoulders full of poisoned arrows, and a powerful bow. Adopting this example, I became a moving arsenal. I walked through the whole Boozie country with my bayonet fixed to my musket, my revolvers belted so as to be seen and feared at the same time, my sword swinging and clanging at my side; and when, to prove my *prestige* in arms, I was asked to fire my revolvers, I would draw and blaze away, several barrels going off almost at the same time—a serious defect, to be sure, but regarded in a very different light by my friends. The bulging fullness of my country coat was attributed to the concealment of similar arms, ready to go off at all points. This swaggering style was not without effect; for it was said that I had money to give my friends and arms to fight my enemies. I had almost forgotten to mention that I was informed by Dowilnyah that five principal chiefs were concerned in the assault on Seymore; that not one of them was now living; that their death was accounted as the punishment of God for this act of wickedness.

Seymore, relaxing all caution on account of the uniform good treatment he had received from the natives, thought them incapable of a different conduct. He was seriously convinced to the contrary. When villainy of this kind is to be perpetrated, the greatest secrecy among those who are privy to it is preserved. It is always the act of a few; for the feelings of the mass seem to be averse to such doings. Seymore's affair was mentioned in terms of reprobation by all who conversed with me about the matter. Comma's own son strenuously denied to me that his father had any part in the matter; though it is a fact notorious throughout the country that his father was a principal actor, and that the whole plot was concocted at the town of Boe.

From Bokkasah we came to Fissahbue, on Monday, the 8th of February, 1869. On Tuesday, the 9th, we arrived at Zolu. King Momoru had not, up to this time, been able to effect a reconciliation between the parties. Every day they made reprisals on each other. While I was there, the Boozies succeeded in capturing several persons belonging to the Barline people. The wars of these people are, however, not attended with any sanguinary results. They consist mostly in surprising a few individuals where they can be suddenly come upon. Sometimes the roads are waylaid wherever their respective traders are supposed to pass. These, together with some other petty annoyances, constitute their principal mode of warfare. The large walled towns are seldom taken. Pitched battles are seldom fought; and even when these people may be said to take the open field, most is done by some war chief by way of displaying his individual prowess. If they were to indulge too much in war, they could never have the numerous and large markets with which their country is everywhere dotted.

Tuesday, the 16th of February, 1869, we started from Zolu, passed through the Boozie towns of Yahwuzue, Kaulitodah, Wuzugabzeah. On the road we met Beah, our Mandingo guide, with some Bokkasah traders, who informed that the Americans had carried war against Manna. We halted at Powlazue. Wednesday, the 17th of February, we passed Zolaghee and its large creek, running over a bed of red feldspar granite. Thousands of fish, known among us as "bonies," were swimming close to shore, not at all annoyed by the people who were bathing in the same water.

We halted at Moffotah. Thursday, the 18th of February, we passed Malang, Ballah, and Dahtazue, and halted at a small village. On Friday, the 19th of February, we reached Barkomah. Saturday, the 20th, leaving Barkomah, we passed through several villages and the town of Nessahbeah. We halted at Sellayo, at six o'clock P.M.

Sunday, the 21st, starting from Sellayo, we passed Barpellum, where we saw a man who had been wounded in four places with a cutlass. He had been beset in the road by some unknown persons; showing, after all, the danger and insecurity of the roads, as well as the folly of traveling unarmed. At four P.M., we reached Totoquella, the residence of King Momoru, where we were received with every demonstration of joy and hospitality. Here we spent some time, in order to avail ourselves of the opportunity of completing calculations of longitude, which, when we were at Boporu, we had been unable to do on account of the weather.

While we were staying at Totoquella, some of the king's people killed an elephant; and instead of beef we had elephant for dinner. The part regarded as a delicacy, and upon which we dined heartily, was the proboscis. He had not yielded his life in a tame, unbecoming manner; his death was attended with the flight of his enemies, the smashing up of gun-stocks, the stamping and rending of saplings. One musket had its barrel literally bent to an angle of ninety degrees. The narrow escape of the hunters themselves suggested to me what might have happened, had I attacked the herd of elephants feeding in the cotton-fields of Ballatah. There the country is open and exposed; here the friendly woods and jungle offer the hunter immediate concealment and protection. The elephants upon the highlands pertinaciously go in herds, and scarcely ever allow themselves to be separated. Intrepid elephant-hunters, accustomed to display firmness and certainty within six paces of a furious charge, are invited to try their prowess with the Ballatah elephants.

www.ingramcontent.com/pod-product-compliance
Lightning Source LLC
Chambersburg PA
CBHW020134170426
43199CB00010B/738